NICO SGARLATO

SOVIET AIRCRAFT OF TODAY

ARMS AND ARMOUR PRESS

Published in 1978 by
Arms and Armour Press,
Lionel Leventhal Ltd.,
2–6 Hampstead High St.,
London NW3 1QQ.

ISBN 0 85368 142 2

Printed in Italy
La Tipografica Parmense

FOREWORD

The Soviet Union's economic and political trends are greatly reflected in its national aeronautics industry which is responsible for supplying a great number of aircraft to numerically the biggest air force in the world. The aircraft used are generally slightly inferior in flexibility compared to those usually seen in the West, and so, a remarkable specialization and also prototyping activity, which has not found equal in other countries for the past twenty years, can be noted. Furthermore, the USSR supplies combat aircraft to the air forces of the Warsaw Pact, allies and friendly nations. Therefore, even though the state's industrial output is comparatively higher than that of the West's, the life span of Soviet aircraft is longer and consequently combat aircraft of various generations can be found in service at the same time (as in the case of the MiG-17, MiG-19, MiG-21 and MiG-23 contemporaneously present in first line units at the end of 1976 and having comparable functions).

The prolonged discussions concerning the presumable qualitative superiority or inferiority of Western versus Eastern aircraft are invalid in as much as a direct comparison cannot be made; however, it is evident that any novelty which comes from the East has a tendency to be initially overrated and then defamed when put into service. Another legend to disprove is the extremely short development periods for Soviet combat aircraft, an illusion due to the fact that the aircraft are made public only after the evaluation and test flights have begun and when they will soon be put into service. Actually many V-VS first line aircraft are the result of very original concepts at the moment of their ideation, but by the time they were distributed to the units (in great numbers), they were already obsolete (at least under certain aspects), by western standards.

The West tends to identify any Soviet air arm with the V-VS (Voenno-Vozhdusni Silii), but a similar differentiation as used in other countries also exists in the USSR; for example, besides the V-VS units for fleet defence and anti-ship attack there are both a naval aviation (the AV-MF), principally equipped with multiengined aircraft of great range, and a real and proper aviation of the fleet equipped with ASW carrierborne helicopters, training and landing helicopters and just recently combat vertical take-off aircraft.

The soviet air forces

Tanks to the ever constant rôle, in recent years, of the USAF strategic reconnaissance satellites and to the information disclosed at the SALT meetings (Strategic Arms Limitation Talks), it is now possible to have a rather accurate and complete picture of the extent of the USSR Air Forces.

Their aviation is appropriately called the Voenno-Vozhdushniye Silii. It consists of approximately one million men (and three million reservs) who are conscripted for 24 months and a number of aircraft estimated at over 10,000-14,500 (these differences are due to the various interpretations given to the definition «combat aircraft»; furthermore, according to some sources, these figures also include army and navy air units). To this must be added 350,000 other men belonging to land-based strategic missile units, various hundreds of thousands of SAM and tactical missile units, crews of approximately 70 missile nuclear submarines, 75,000 men of the Aviatsiya Voenno-Morskovo Flota (AV-MF, the naval aviation) and 10,000 men in the coastal missile units.

The V-VS, commanded by Marshal Pavel Stepanovich Kutahov, is subdivided into five autonomous commands: P-VO Strany (Protivo-Vozhdushnava

The Mikoyan MiG-9FR (Fargo) was claimed to be the first Russian jet fighter.

The Sukhoi Su-11 (not to be confused with the Flagon) was inspired by the German Me.262.

A Yakovlev Yak-17 (Feather) jet fighter intended for the Czech air force but eventually discarded.

Oborona Strany, Homeland Air Defense), FA (Frontovaya Aviatsiya, «Front-line» or Tactical Air Force), DA or ADD (Dalnaya Aviatsiya or Aviatsiya Dal'nevo Deistviya, Long Range or Strategic Air Force), MA or AV-MF (Morskaya Aviatsiya or Aviatsiya Voenno-Morskovo Flota, Naval Aviation), and V-TA (Voenno-Transportnaya Aviatsiya, Military Transport Air Force).

The Air Defence Command (P-VO)
The P-VO (Strany), 500,000 men strong, is, numerically, the most important branch of the Soviet Air Forces and all surface-to-air defence depends on it; from the radar early warning, to the strategic reconnaissance satellites, to the surface-to-air missiles or SAM and anti-ballistic missiles or ABM, and to the interceptors. From 1948 this enormous complex of men and equipment has been under the orders of a unified command, with headquarters in Moscow, and its autority does not only come from the Supreme Headquarters of the Air Force but also from the Self-defence Nuclear Strategic Force.

All the territory of the Soviet Union is divided into 16 Air Defence Districts: 9 in European Russia (the districts of Leningrad, the Baltic, the Bielorussia, the Carpathians, Kiev, Moscow, Odessa, Northern Caucasus and Trans Caucasia), 3 in Central Russia (the Urals, the Volga, Tashkent and Turkestan) with strategic reserve functions and 4 in Asiatic Russia (Transbaikal, Central Asia, Siberia and the Far East). Six other air defence districts correspond to the 6 other countries of the Warsaw Pact (East Germany, Czechoslovakia, Poland, Hunagry, Romania and Bulgaria); the other «satellite state» of the USSR, Mongolia, comes under the air cover of the Transbaikal district. The early warning and control centres are deeply dislocated internally in the country and are in constant contact with the operational units of all the countries which are members of the alliance.

The IAP-VO (Strany) or Istrebitel'naya Aviatsiya P-VO Strany (Fighter Command of the PVO Strany) is part of the PV-O (Strany), which is composed of «eskadrilii» (flights) of 12 aircraft (generally nine or ten single-seaters and two two-seaters for

The Mikoyan-Gurevich MiG-15 bis (Fagot-B) was in the same class of US F-86 Sabre. In the picture a North Korean aircraft.

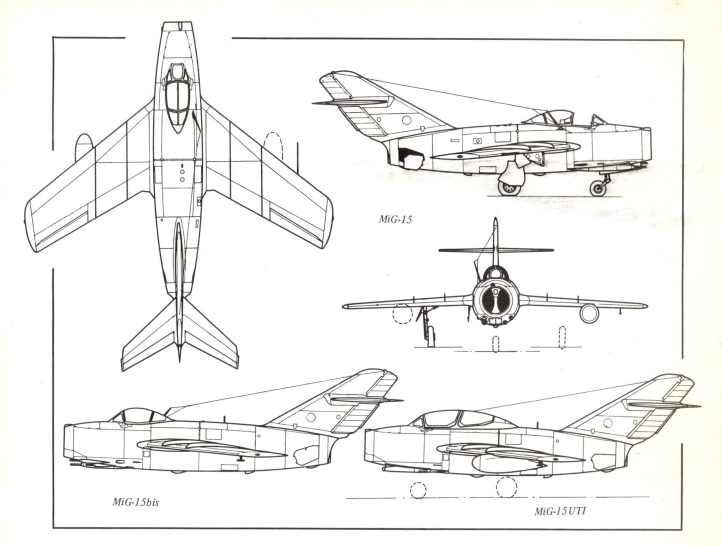

MiG-15

MiG-15bis

MiG-15UTI

operational proficiency training); three flights make up a «polk» (regiment) and three or more regiments form a «divisiya» (division), the principal unit.

The IAP-VO has, at its disposal, 2,600 first line interceptor fighters made up of approximately 500-935 Sukhoi Su-15s (in Flagon-A, -C, -D, and -E version), 200 Mikoyan MiG-25Ps (Foxbat-A), 130-400 Tupolev TU-28Ps (Fiddler-B) presently being replaced, beginning in 1974, with a substantially lesser number (50?) of Tupolev Tu-22P (Blinder-E) as strategic interceptors, approximately 300 Sukhoi Su-11s (Fishpot-C) for short range defence, together with approximately 800-850 Yakovlev Yak-28P (Firebar) and Mikoyan MiG-19PM (Farmer-E).

A Czech Air Force MiG-17PF (Fresco-D) the main night fighter version. The MiG-17 differed from the MiG-15 bis (below, right) mainly for the wing planform and the more powerful engine.

The PV-O also has its own transport and liaison units on Antonov An-12 (Cub) and Ilyushin Il-14 (Crate), however almost completely replaced with the more modern Antonov An-26 (Curl), distributed at division level, while liaisons are still partly

The Mikoyan-Gurevich MiG-17PFU (Fresco-E) night fighter with all-missile armament.

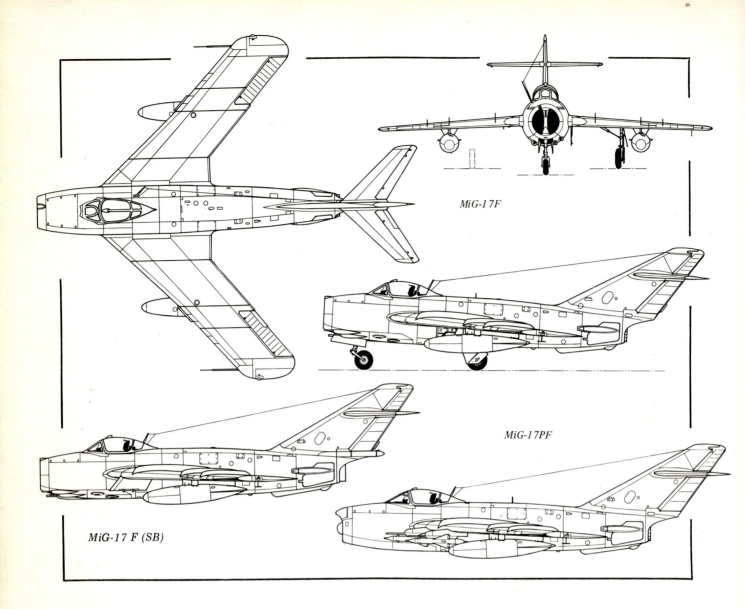

MiG-17F

MiG-17PF

MiG-17 F (SB)

carried out by the old Antonov An-2 (Colt) biplanes partially replaced by some An-14 Pchelka (Clod), both destined to be replaced by the new An-28. Ten Tupolev Tu-126s (Moss) ensures radar early warning and airborne control for the interceptors.

In addition to flight units there are missile units: 64 silos for antimissile ABM-1 Galosh missiles located around Moscow, sustained by early warning radars Hen House, Try Add for target identification and Dog House for target control, more than 12,000 launching rails in 1,650 bases, with 3,200 SA-1 Guild missiles, 3,400 V-750VK (SA-2 Guideline Mk. 3, 4 and 6) with Fan Song radar, 3,700 SA-3 Goa Mk.1 and Mk.2 with Low Blow radar also with new four rail launchers, 1,800 SA-5 Gammon with limited anti-missile capability in association with different types of radar; besides there are the SA-4 Ganef with Pat Hand radar and the SA-6 Gainful Mk.1 and Mk.2 with Straight Flush radar of the field mobile units.

The Yakovlev Yak-25P (Flashlight-A) twin jet was representative of the all-weather first generation.

The Yak-25R (Flashlight-B) was a tactical reconnaissance derivative.

The Tactical Air Command

The Frontovaya Aviatsiya, command for V-VS, has, at its disposal, the largest number of aircraft, 3,350, with which it must ensure close air support for the land forces, interdiction and counter-air on the battlefield and destruction of enemy aircraft on land or in flight (local air superiority). It is subdivided into 15 Air Forces of the Guard, each of which has from one to nine units. An exception is the unit assigned to East Germany which is subdivided into five air corps of two of three divisions. The FA «polki» have a variable structure according to their roles: 40 fighters, 35 light bombers, 32 light transport aircraft, 36 medium transport aircraft, 30 reconnaissance aircraft or 36 helicopters.

Each air force is operatively subordinated to a military district command. The FA's total number of combat aircraft includes 500 Mikoyan MiG-23s and MiG-27s in Flogger B-C-D versions, approximately 200 reconnaissance MiG-25Rs (Foxbat-B), about 100 (the number should increase) Sukhoi Su-17s (Fitter-C) light bombers, 50-55 Su-19s (Fencer-A) in the class of the US F-111, approximately 200 Yakovlev Yak-28s (Brewer) reconnaissance and electronic warfare versions (Brewer-E), less popular with the arrival of the Su-17 and -19, 400 Sukhoi Su-7s (Fitter-A) and 1,700 Mikoyan MiG-21PFMs, PFMAs, SMTs, etc., (Fishbed-F, -H, -J, -K, -L, -N, etc.). In addition there are 600 MiG-17Fs and over 400 second line aircraft including the MiG-19SF, Su-7B of the first type, Il-28, Yak-27R and Il-28U.

The total number of helicopters varies, according to different estimates, between 600 and 2,000. They are primarily made up of Mil Mi-4 or V-4, from different versions of the V-8 and of the V-6.

The strategic Air Command (ADD)

The ADD or DA, directly under the Nuclear Strategic Forces Command (offensive), is subdivided into three air forces; two located near the western frontier and the other in the far east. It has, in its ranks, approximately 900 combat aircraft. Among these there are 100 Tupolev Tu-20s (Bear-B) armed with AS-3 Kangaroo missiles and 35 Myasischev M-4s (Bison-C), 35-50 M-4s (Bison-B) tankers and 450 Tupolev TU-16s (Badger-A) medium bombers also used for training in in-flight refuelling, in addition several hundred reserve and strategic reconnaissance models and 175 Tupolev Tu-22 (Blinder) bombers and electronic warfare aircraft. The Tupolev Backfire-B swing wing strategic bombers are increasingly used alongside them.

The Naval Aviation (AV-MF)

The Soviet Naval Aviation, under the command of the four «Red Flag» Fleets of the Baltic (headquarters in Kaliningrad), the North (headquarters in Severomorsk), the Black Sea (headquarters in Sevastopol) and the Far East and Pacific (headquarters in Vladivostok), avails itself of approximately 75,000 men and about 1,200 aircraft which include 50 Tu-20s (Bear-C, -D, -E

and -F) for strategic reconnaissance and missile guidance, 125 Tu-16s (Badger-D, -E, -F) for strategic reconnaissance, 300 Tu-16s (Badger-G), 200 of which are used in the Black Sea Fleet as bombers, for missile attack and in-flight refuelling, 50-55 Tu-22s (Blinder-A and -C), 40 Yak-28s (Brewer) light bombers, 80 Il-38s (May) ASW patrol aircraft, 100 Beriev Be-12s Tchaika (Mail) ASW amphibious flying boats, several M-4 tankers, TU-126s (Moss) early warning aircraft, approximately 200 transport and liaison aircraft of various types and 270 helicopters made up of V-4 (Hound), rapidly being phased-out, V-24 (Hind-B), V-14 (Haze), Ka-25 (Hormone-A), V-8 (Hip) and V-6 (Hook), 40 of which, all Ka-25, are stationed on board the helicopter carriers *Moskva* and *Leningrad* (20 per unit), and 13, one per unit, on three *Nikolajev (Kara)* class cruisers, on four *Admiral Drouzd (Kresta I)* class cruisers, and on six *Admiral Isakov (Kresta II)*. In addition, on board the two aircraft carriers *Kiev* class (Kuril), there are approximately 48 Ka-25, a certain number of V-14 (Haze) and at least 24-30 new Yakovlev Yak-36 (Forger) V/STOL fighter bombers.

The Transport Command (V-TA)

The Military Transport Air Force Command, principally set up to assist the strategic reserve and the eight divisions of air transport troops, has approximately 1,700 aeroplanes (which include 700-900 Antonov An-24s, An-26s and An-30s and probably the new An-32 will be added, replacing the Ilyushin Il-14, 600-800 Antonov An-12s and

One of the major achievements of the Soviet aircraft industry in the light bomber field was the Ilyushin IL-28 (Beagle). The aircraft coded 842 belongs to the Indonesian Air Force.

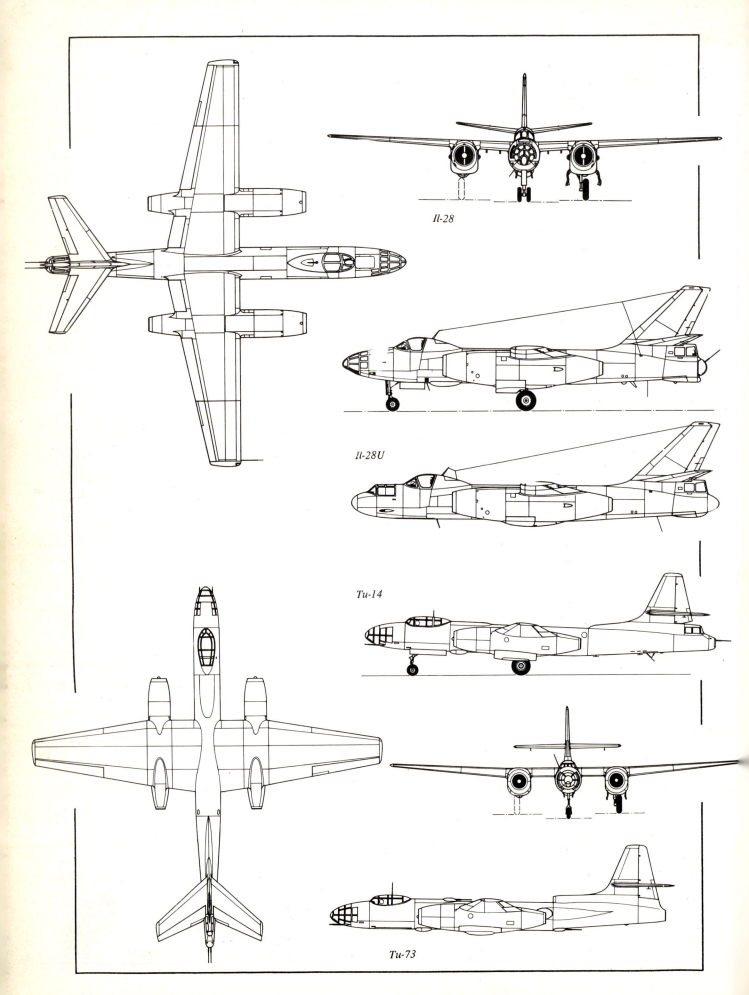

Il-28

Il-28U

Tu-14

Tu-73

between 12 to 60 An-22s, the Il-76 are being put into service and, in the future, should flank the An-40), and 1,200-2,000 helicopters (approximately 500 V-4s, 500 V-6s, and V-10 and the remainder made up of V-1, V-2, V-8 and V-12). The V-TA avails itself of several Il-18, Il-62, An-24 and Yak-40 for passenger and VIP transport and government duties, while in the event of air lifts it can obtain approximately 100 four-turboprop Antonovs, and other types of aircraft (including the An-22) from the Aeroflot.

Training

With the exception of the DOSAAF, a paramilitary corps which furnishes *ab initio* training principally utilizing Yakovlev Yak-18 (Max) and Yak-11 (Moose) and Mil V-1U (Hare) helicopters, Soviet cadet pilots attend «all jet» courses in the numerous flight schools and academies throughout the country. There are three aeronautic academies: the *N. E. Zukovsky* located in both Moscow and Schcelkovo (near the capital), the *Yu. A. Gagarin* of Monino (where an aeronautic museum is also located), near Schcelkovo and north-west of Moscow, with courses for commanding officers (CO) and staff officers and VIRTA the *L. A. Govorov* Academy of Radiotechnology in Kharkov.

Among other schools there are the A. F. Myasnikov, the largest in the world, located in Volgograd, the Senior School for Pilots, with two separate bases and the Senior School for Pilots and Navigators in Stavropol. In addition there are approximately 15 operational conversion units and specialization schools.

The flight equipment is extremely standardized and it is composed of approximately 2,000 Czechoslovakian-made Aero L-29 Delfin which are progressively being replaced, beginning in 1974, with the more modern L-39 Albatross. From these the pilot moves on to the MiG-15U (Midget) and after proceeds to the various operative two-seaters which, in the case of future fighter pilots,

Above to below: the first MiG-21M (Fishbed-J), Indian-built version. A Su-7 (Fitter-A) fitted with ATO rockets. A late-production Su-15 (Flagon-A) with larger tail warning radar. An early MiG-25R (Foxbat-B) strategic reconnaissance aircraft.

are the MiG-21U (Mongol), MiG-23U (Flogger-C), Su-7U (Moujik), Su-9/11U (Maiden), MiG-25U (Foxbat-C) and Su-15U (Flagon-C).

Minor air units

The KGB (State Security Committee) also includes the Border Guards (over 175,000 strong) and real and proper military départments which can also avail themselves of air liaison units, border patrol and logistic support equipped with a great number of helicopters, principally V-4 and V-8, and An-2 and An-14 aircraft.

Colour and markings

Up to the present time, the majority of Soviet combat aircraft has been overall silver/aluminum with only a few exceptions for aircraft camouflaged in dark green (similar to the English dark green) on the upper half and light blue on the lower half (and sometimes light greyish-blue, white or unpainted). This simple camouflage livery was a characteristic of the AV-MF aircraft and it is still common practice with the army and the DOSAAF (a paramilitary organ). Finally, in 1976, a similar camouflage reappeared on the Tupolev Backfire presumably belonging to an experimental unit of the AV-MF. Various camouflages have also been employed for tactical aircraft as the Su-7, MiG-23, and the V-24 helicopters. Instead, shipborne aircraft are grey (those with rotary wings), similar to those of the American and Italian Navy or light greyish-blue (those with fixed wings), similar to the French Aéronavale Etendards.

The nationality markings are formed by a red star with a red spaced outline (the background is usually white, but it can also be the colour of the aircraft), and they always appear on the two sides of the fin while they are no longer repeated on the fuselage. Generally, there are four other stars on the wings, but examples of other combinations can often be seen where the wing markings appear only on the top or on the bottom, on only the left wing or are altogether left out.

ASCC/NATO Designation System

The Soviet Defence Minister has always considered the project, construction and service names of their own aircraft secret and, in general, it only reveals those (often fictitious) in aircraft employed in establishing records (in as much as this is imposed by the Fédération Aéronautique Internationale), or those that are already known (above all when the aircraft referred to are known abroad). For this reason, for the first ten years after the war, the aircraft of the East were identified with progressive numbers. It seems, however, that not all numbers were assigned so as not to reveal how many models were made public. In 1954 the Air Standards Co-ordinating Committee, made up of Australia, Canada, Great Britain, New Zealand and the United States, suggested a new system to the NATO. It was derived from the

one used during the War in the Pacific to identify Japanese aircraft. The system provides for the assignment of names, always in English, more or less derogatory, or at least humourous and rarely do they have a comprehensible relationship to the designated aircraft. The criteria used to assign these names in unknown.

The ASCC system assigns monosyllabic names to piston-engined aircraft and disyllabic to jet propelled aircraft (helicopters are an exception); these nicknames begin with B for bombers, C for cargo aircraft, F for fighters, H for helicopters and M for miscellaneous. The following versions of a specific model are indicated alphabetically by suffix. Below is a list of the names assigned:

Type 1	Yakovlev Yak-15
Type 2	Mikoyan-Gurevich MiG-9
Type 7	Yakovlev Yak-19
Type 8	Lavochkin La-150
Type 9	Tupolev Tu-77
Type 10	Ilyushin Il-22
Type 12	Tupolev Tu-73
Type 14	Mikoyan-Gurevich MiG-15
Type 15	Lavochkin La-15
Type 16	Yakovlev Yak-17UTI
Type 20	Mikoyan-Gurevich MiG-15 (derived versions)
Type 21	Lavochkin La-15UTI
Type 26	Yakovlev Yak-17
Type 27	Ilyushin Il-28
Type 28	Yakovlev Yak-23
Type 29	Mikoyan-Gurevich MiG-15UTI
Type 30	Tupolev Tu-14UTB
Type 31	Tupolev Tu-85
Type 32	Mil Mi-1
Type 35	Tupolev Tu-14
Type 36	Mil Mi-4
Type 37	Myasischev M-4
Type 39	Tupolev Tu-16
Type 40	Tupolev Tu-20

Bombers

Backfin	Tupolev Tu-98
Backfire	Tupolev Tu-26/30 (?)
Badger	Tupolev Tu-16 (Tu-88)
Bank	North American B-25 Mitchell
Barge	Tupolev Tu-85
Bark	Ilyushin Il-2 Shturmovik
Bat	Tupolev Tu-2/6
Beagle	Ilyushin Il-28
Bear	Tupolev Tu-20 (Tu-95)
Beast	Ilyushin Il-10 Shturmovik
Beauty	Tupolev Tu-22 (Tu-105), later replaced as too laudatory
Big Swinger	Spurious name of Tupolev Tu-26/30 (?)
Bison	Myasischev M/Mya-4
Blinder	Tupolev Tu-28 (Tu-102) when erroneously identified as bomber
Blinder	Tupolev Tu-22 (Tu-105)
Blowlamp	Ilyushin Il-54
Bob	Ilyushin Il-4
Boot	Tupolev Tu-91 Tarzan (Bichok)

Bosun	Tupolev Tu-14 (Tu-89)
Bounder	Myasischev M-50/52
Box	Douglas DB-7 A-20 Havoc
Brassard	Yakovlev Yak-28, later Brewer to avoid confusion with the French Broussard
Brawny	Ilyushin Il-40
Brewer	Yakovlev Yak-28
Buck	Petlyakov Pe-2
Buick	Petlyakov Pe-2, later replaced by Buck because it was too laudatory
Bull	Tupolev Tu-4 (Boeing B-29)
Butcher	Tupolev Tu-82 mistakenly also ascribed to the Ilyushin Il-28 and then no longer in use as it could be confused with Badger

Cargo
Cab	Lisunov Li-2 (Douglas DC-3)
Camber	Ilyushin Il-86
Camel	Tupolev Tu-104
Camp	Antonov An-8
Candid	Ilyushin Il-76
Careless	Tupolev Tu-154
Cart	Tupolev Tu-70/75
Cat	Antonov An-10 Ukraina
Charger	Tupolev Tu-144
Clam	Ilyushin Il-18 (1947)
Clank	Antonov An-30
Classic	Ilyushin Il-62
Cleat	Tupolev Tu-114 Rossiya
Clobber	Yakovlev Yak-42
Clod	Antonov An-14 Pchelka
Clog	Antonov An-28 (An-14M)
Coach	Ilyushin Il-12
Cock	Antonov An-22 Antei
Codling	Yakovlev Yak-40
Coke	Antonov An-24
Colt	Antonov An-2/4/6 Kolkozhnik
Cooker	Tupolev Tu-110
Cookpot	Tupolev Tu-124
Coot	Ilyushin Il-18
Cork	Yakovlev Yak-16
Crate	Ilyushin Il-14
Creek	Yakovlev Yak-12
Crib	Yakovlev Yak-6
Crow	Yakovlev Yak-10
Crusty	Tupolev Tu-134
Cub	Antonov An-12
Cuff	Beriev Be-30
Curl	Antonov An-26

Fighters
Faceplate	Mikoyan E-2A
Fagot	Mikoyan-Gurevich MiG-15
Faithless	Mikoyan E-230
Falcon	Mikoyan-Gurevich MiG-15; later replaced because it was too laudatory
Fang	Lavochkin La-11
Fantail	Lavochkin La-17
Fargo	Mikoyan-Gurevich MiG-9
Farmer	Mikoyan MiG-19
Fencer	Sukhoi Su-19

Fearless	Advanced Soviet Fighter variable geometry twin-jet hypothesized by the USAF to be inserted in the software of the flight simulators
Feather	Yakovlev Yak-17
Fiddler	Tupolev Tu-28 (Tu-102)
Fin	Lavochkin La-7
Firebar	Yakovlev Yak-27
Fishbed	Mikoyan MiG-21
Fishpot	Sukhoi Su-9/11
Fitter	Sukhoi Su-7/17/20/22
Flagon	Sukhoi Su-15
Flashlight	Yakovlev Yak-25
Flipper	Mikoyan E/I-152
Flogger	Mikoyan MiG-23/27 (E-231)
Flora	Yakovlev Yak-23
Forger	Yakovlev Yak-36 (?)
Foxbat	Mikoyan MiG-25 (E-266)
Frank	Yakovlev Yak-9
Fred	Bell P-63 Kingcobra
Freehand	Yakovlev Yak-34 (?)
Fresco	Mikoyan-Gurevich MiG-17
Fritz	Lavochkin La-9
Frosty	Tupolev Tu-10/72 or a supposed fighter version of the Brawny

Helicopters
Hare	Mil Mi-1/V-1 (Moskvich)
Harke	Mil Mi-10
Harp	Kamov Ka-20
Hat	Kamov Ka-10
Haze	Mil Mi-14
Hen	Kamov Ka-15
Hind	Mil Mi-24
Hip	Mil Mi-8/V-8
Hog	Kamov Ka-18
Homer	Mil Mi-12/V-12
Hoodlum	Kamov Ka-26
Hook	Mil Mi-6/V-6
Hoop	Kamov Ka-22 Vintokrulya
Hoplite	Mil Mi-2
Hormone	Kamov Ka-25
Horse	Yakovlev Yak-24
Hound	Mil Mi-4/V-4

Miscellaneous
Madge	Beriev Be-6
Maestro	Yakovlev Yak-28U
Magnet	Yakovlev Yak-17
Magnum	Yakovlev Yak-30
Maiden	Sukhoi Su-9U
Mail	Beriev Be-12/M-12
Mallow	Beriev Be-10/M-10
Mandrake	Yakovlev Yak-26 (RV)
Mangrove	Yakovlev Yak-27R
Mantis	Yakovlev Yak-32
Mare	Yakovlev Yak-14 (glider)
Mark	Yakovlev Yak-7U (UTI-26)
Mascot	Ilyushin Il-28U
Max	Yakovlev Yak-18
May	Ilyushin Il-38
Maya	Aero L-29 Delfin
Midget	Mikoyan-Gurevich MiG-15UTI

Mink	Yakovlev UT-2	Moss	Tupolev Tu-126
Mist	Tsibin Ts-25	Mote	Beriev Be-2
Mole	Beriev Be-8	Moujik	Sukhoi Su-7U
Mongol	Mikoyan MiG-21U	Mouse	Yakovlev Yak-18M
Moose	Yakovlev Yak-11	Mug	Chetverikov Che-2 MDR-6
Mop	Amtorg/Taganrog GST/MP-7 (Conso- lidated 28 Catalina)	Mule	Polikarpov Po-2 Kukuruznik

---

Mikoyan MiG-19 (Farmer)

The Mikoyan MiG-19 has been defined «the Super Sabre of the Iron Curtain», and without a doubt it has been one of the longest lived fighter-bombers ever created by Mikoyan (as well as the first to be designed without the help of Guverich and the last to bear the Istrebitel service name, fighter or «destroyer»). It was produced by three different countries, almost uninterruptedly, from 1953 to 1971: the USSR, Czechoslovakia and China. Today the MiG-19 is still being built in China, alternating with the MiG-21 on the assembly lines, and has given life to an improved version, the F-9.

The success of this aircraft is due to many factors, in particular a certain flexibility which finds little comparison with other Soviet combat aircraft, even subsequent ones.

In the West, even as late as the mid 1950's, this aircraft was ignored or confused with the Mikoyan MiG-17SN and 1-320 (R-1) and the Lavochkin La-160, although its construction had already been ordered on July 30, 1951, when it was evident that this project was far superior to its competitors: the Yakovlev Yak-1000, Lavochkin La-190 and the Mikoyan-Gurevich I-350 (single-engined with a turbojet Lyulka AL-5). Therefore, for western observers, the MiG-19 unexpectedly appeared in the 1955 Tushino Air Show in which no fewer than 48 aircraft of this type took part.

The MiG-19 did not follow the logical line of development of the MiG-15 and MiG-17 because of the poor reliability of the Lyulka turbojet and it rather bears the marks of the MiG-9. Its design was inspired by a government request to create

Above: the Mikoyan MiG-19F (Farmer-A) standard day fighter. Here: the MiG-19PF (Farmer-B) limited all-weather fighter.

the «fastest fighter in the world», a requirement, therefore, very similar to that which produced the U.S. North American F-100 and the Lockheed F-104.

The MiG-19PM (Farmer-E) was the all-missile version.

Mikoyan MiG-19F (Farmer-C) cutaway drawing key

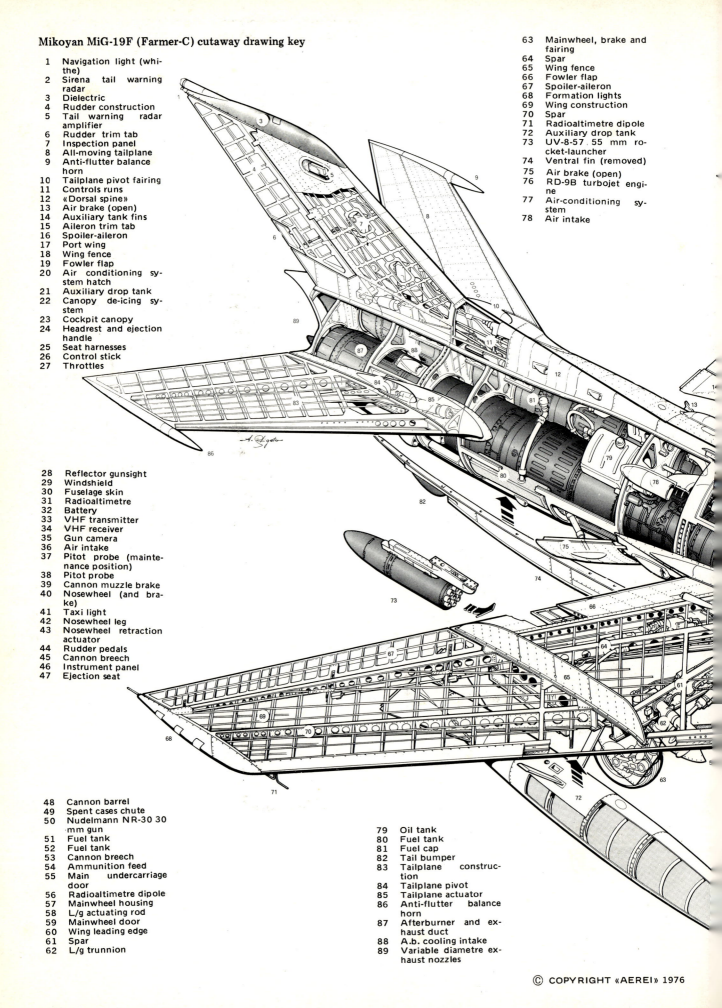

1   Navigation light (white)
2   Sirena tail warning radar
3   Dielectric
4   Rudder construction
5   Tail warning radar amplifier
6   Rudder trim tab
7   Inspection panel
8   All-moving tailplane
9   Anti-flutter balance horn
10 Tailplane pivot fairing
11 Controls runs
12 «Dorsal spine»
13 Air brake (open)
14 Auxiliary tank fins
15 Aileron trim tab
16 Spoiler-aileron
17 Port wing
18 Wing fence
19 Fowler flap
20 Air conditioning system hatch
21 Auxiliary drop tank
22 Canopy de-icing system
23 Cockpit canopy
24 Headrest and ejection handle
25 Seat harnesses
26 Control stick
27 Throttles

28 Reflector gunsight
29 Windshield
30 Fuselage skin
31 Radioaltimetre
32 Battery
33 VHF transmitter
34 VHF receiver
35 Gun camera
36 Air intake
37 Pitot probe (maintenance position)
38 Pitot probe
39 Cannon muzzle brake
40 Nosewheel (and brake)
41 Taxi light
42 Nosewheel leg
43 Nosewheel retraction actuator
44 Rudder pedals
45 Cannon breech
46 Instrument panel
47 Ejection seat

48 Cannon barrel
49 Spent cases chute
50 Nudelmann NR-30 30 mm gun
51 Fuel tank
52 Fuel tank
53 Cannon breech
54 Ammunition feed
55 Main undercarriage door
56 Radioaltimetre dipole
57 Mainwheel housing
58 L/g actuating rod
59 Mainwheel door
60 Wing leading edge
61 Spar
62 L/g trunnion

63 Mainwheel, brake and fairing
64 Spar
65 Wing fence
66 Fowler flap
67 Spoiler-aileron
68 Formation lights
69 Wing construction
70 Spar
71 Radioaltimetre dipole
72 Auxiliary drop tank
73 UV-8-57 55 mm rocket-launcher
74 Ventral fin (removed)
75 Air brake (open)
76 RD-9B turbojet engine
77 Air-conditioning system
78 Air intake

79 Oil tank
80 Fuel tank
81 Fuel cap
82 Tail bumper
83 Tailplane construction
84 Tailplane pivot
85 Tailplane actuator
86 Anti-flutter balance horn
87 Afterburner and exhaust duct
88 A.b. cooling intake
89 Variable diametre exhaust nozzles

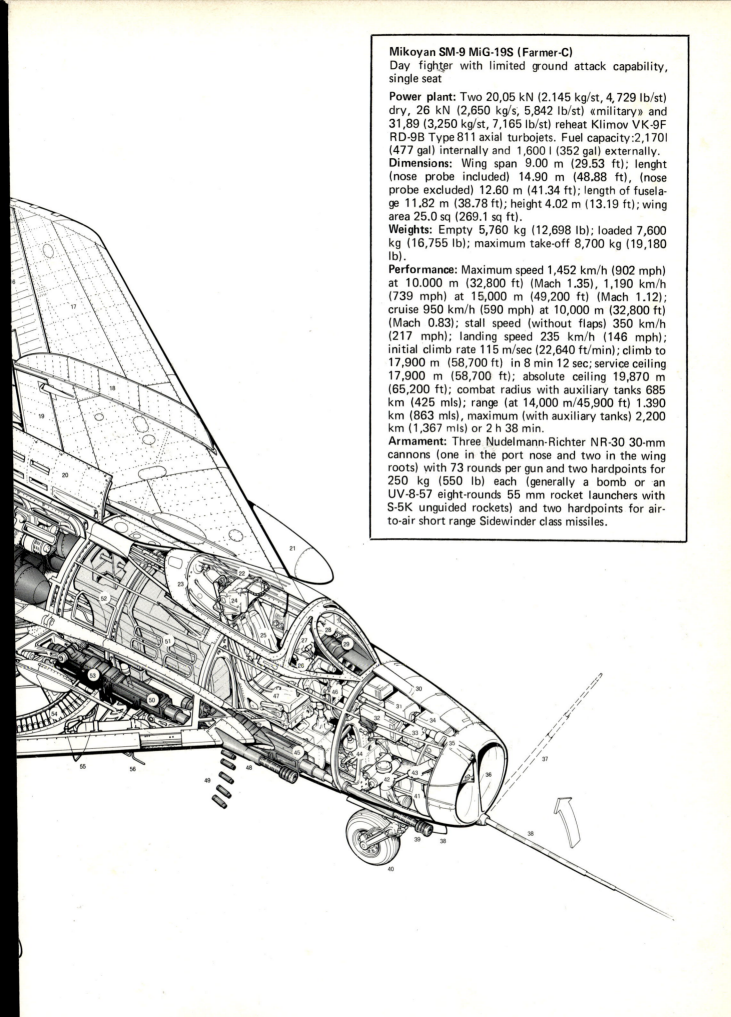

Mikoyan SM-9 MiG-19S (Farmer-C)
Day fighter with limited ground attack capability, single seat

Power plant: Two 20,05 kN (2.145 kg/st, 4,729 lb/st) dry, 26 kN (2,650 kg/s, 5,842 lb/st) «military» and 31,89 (3,250 kg/st, 7,165 lb/st) reheat Klimov VK-9F RD-9B Type 811 axial turbojets. Fuel capacity : 2,170l (477 gal) internally and 1,600 l (352 gal) externally.
Dimensions: Wing span 9.00 m (29.53 ft); lenght (nose probe included) 14.90 m (48.88 ft), (nose probe excluded) 12.60 m (41.34 ft); length of fuselage 11.82 m (38.78 ft); height 4.02 m (13.19 ft); wing area 25.0 sq (269.1 sq ft).
Weights: Empty 5,760 kg (12,698 lb); loaded 7,600 kg (16,755 lb); maximum take-off 8,700 kg (19,180 lb).
Performance: Maximum speed 1,452 km/h (902 mph) at 10.000 m (32,800 ft) (Mach 1.35), 1,190 km/h (739 mph) at 15,000 m (49,200 ft) (Mach 1.12); cruise 950 km/h (590 mph) at 10,000 m (32,800 ft) (Mach 0.83); stall speed (without flaps) 350 km/h (217 mph); landing speed 235 km/h (146 mph); initial climb rate 115 m/sec (22,640 ft/min); climb to 17,900 m (58,700 ft) in 8 min 12 sec; service ceiling 17,900 m (58,700 ft); absolute ceiling 19,870 m (65,200 ft); combat radius with auxiliary tanks 685 km (425 mls); range (at 14,000 m/45,900 ft) 1.390 km (863 mls), maximum (with auxiliary tanks) 2,200 km (1,367 mls) or 2 h 38 min.
Armament: Three Nudelmann-Richter NR-30 30-mm cannons (one in the port nose and two in the wing roots) with 73 rounds per gun and two hardpoints for 250 kg (550 lb) each (generally a bomb or an UV-8-57 eight-rounds 55 mm rocket launchers with S-5K unguided rockets) and two hardpoints for air-to-air short range Sidewinder class missiles.

Above: a Czech Air Force Farmer-C. Below: the protruding left wing Nudelmann-Richter NR-30 30 mm cannon.

Above: line-up of F-6s being serviced by Pakistani ground crewmen. Below: the tremendous punch of the 30 mm trio.

Thanks to the availability of the compact Mikulin 19.62 kN AM-5 (2,000 kg/st, 4,409 lb/st) turbojet Mikoyan and Gurevich's OKB (Opytno-Konstruktorskoye Byuro, Experimental Design Bureau) decided, private venture, to adapt the traditional circular cross section fuselage of the I-350 to the two engines, placed side by side in the tail. The set of cannons contained in the nose of the MiG-17 was substituted with a gun in the nose and two wing-mounted ones so that the firing exhausts would not affect the flux through the air intake.

The first I-360 prototype flew, for the first time, in 1952 and in September of the same year, (according to other sources in 1953), was followed by the I-350M piloted by Major Grigori Sedov.

The first version of a pre-series MiG-19F (Farmer-A) with two 21.34 KN turbojets (2,175 kg/s, 4,795 lb.st) dry and 29.83 kN (3,040 kg/s, 6,702 lb/st) with reheat (Mikulin AM-5F followed the year after. This involved a day fighter configuration, armed with two 23 mm NR-23 and one 37 mm N-37 cannons. Then followed the MiG-19PF (Farmer-B, also known as the «limited all-weather Farmer»), featuring an extended nose to accomodate a Izumrud (Emerald) search and intercept radar developed in co-operation with the Czech industry.

During the first period of use the MiG-19F and 19PF revealed a few troublesome inconveniences with regards to controls. Therefore, on the assembly line the MiG-19S (Farmer-C) with all-moving slab type tailplanes evolved. During production the MiG-19S (briefly also known as the MiG-19SF) also underwent replacement of the original motors with the Klimov VK-9 F/RD-9B and the armament was replaced with three Nudelmann-Richter 30 mm NR-30 cannons recognized by their big muzzle brake. A variation with limited all-weather performance was also produced with the installation of a RP-5 Izumrud (Scan Odd) radar and of a Sirena tail warning radar, called Farmer-D. A two seater MiG-19UTI model was also constructed but in very small quantities.

The final mass-produced version, was the MiG-19PM (Farmer-E) in which all the cannons

The Shenyang F-6 (in Pakistani colours) is the Chinese-built version of the Farmer-C.

MiG-19S (Farmer-C), Soviet V-VS, circa 1966. The aircraft belongs to an aerobatic team.

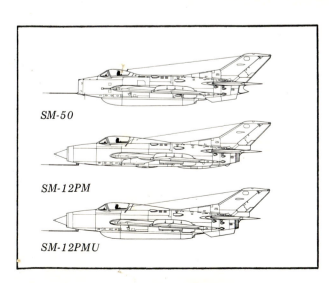

SM-50

SM-12PM

SM-12PMU

were removed and the arming was exclusively made up of four radar homing K-5M (AA-1 Alkali) missiles. The MiG-19PM remained in service in first line units until 1969 and in second line units until 1971-72. Farmer-C, instead, served in the tactical aviation until 1973 and was then progressively assigned to secondary units and training use.

Other noteworthy versions are: the F-6, built in China in the Shenyang plant; the reconnaissance MiG-19R with two cameras in place of the central cannon, the SM-10 with probe for in-flight refuelling, the SM-12PM with fire control similar to

that of the MiG-21, with armament made up of two K-5M, two Tumansky RZ-26 turbojets, the SM-12PMU, same as the above but with two RZM-26 motors and an auxiliary Dushkin RU-01S rocket, the SM-30 for take-off tests with catapults, the SM-50, modified in 1959 by the installation of two RD-9BM motors and an auxiliary U-19 rocket by which it could reach a maximum speed of Mach 1.8, the F-9, a version of the F-6 produced in China with R2L radar and modified forward fuselage: the MiG-19SV, specialized point interceptor version powered by two RD-9BF engines, with modified afterburner and intended to run continuously on full reheat: endurance was of only 25 minutes and TBO was restricted at 75 hours.

Recently the Chinese and Pakistans have, in addition to the NR-30 cannons, mounted two K-13A (AA-2 Atoll) missiles on the day versions and the MiG-19 fought very well in the last Indo-Pakistan conflict shooting down eight Sukhoi Su-7, three Hunters and one MiG-21.

The starboard mainwheel housing and an UV-7-57 55 mm light rocket launcher in a Czech Farmer-C.

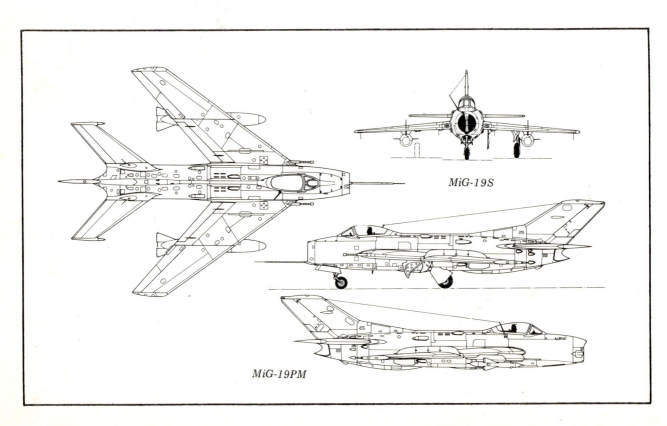

MiG-19S

MiG-19PM

Mikoyan MiG-21 (Fishbed)

Without a doubt, the Mikoyan MiG-21 is not only the most famous Soviet fighter of the last 30 years but also the one produced in major quantity and furnished to almost all the USSR's friendly nations.

In 1953 the V-VS issued a detailed requirement for an air superiority fighter (even if this definition was not used in the USSR and it was referred to as a «short range interceptor fighter»). The Artem Ivanovich Mikoyan Engineering Staff replied to the request by presenting a tailed delta called E-5 and this aircraft was shown to the public for the first time during Aviation Day in Tushino (near Moscow) on June 24, 1956. In the West it was referred to as Fishbed.

After approval of the project a small number of exemplars were produced, possibly only three, and called MiG-21 (Fishbed-A). They were powered by an RD-11 Tumansky turbojet.

The single-seat MiG-21 belongs to the first Soviet generation of «Mach 2» fighters and in many respects it is comparable to the American F-104 Starfighter and the French Mirage III. Its construction is rather simple if not coarse in certain aspects.

The instruments are made up of an R1L (High Fix-A) fire control or of the improved R2L (High Fix-B) version which operates with a scanning beam that can be oriented and two pulse repetition frequencies (PFR); one between 825 and 950 pulses/sec for search and one which goes from 1,750 to 1,850 pulses/sec to «tracked» target. The system has a maximum power of 100 kW and the range is more than 30 km. The so called «third generation» MiG-21s can operate, connected via «data link», in place of the airborne warning and control Tupolev Tu-126 aircraft even if more recently conceived types are preferred as interceptors.

Ground information (or airborne control information) is received through a secure Markham (NATO code) communication system. According to the model, three types of seats have been adopted. The cockpit is pressurized and the pilot is always provided with the most recent retroscope system and a windscreen which is fireproofed against small calibre arms. Among the flight instruments, comparable to those in the West, the VOR/ADF navigation system and the tail warning radar with a 45° scanning area should be mentioned.

The Mikoyan 152 (Flipper) was a prototype that failed to replace the MiG-21.

Above: the prototype of the MiG-21PF (Fishbed-D), first limited all-weather version. Below: the MiG-21 bis (Fishbed-L or -M) is the latest version with the uprated Tumansky R-25 engine.

Mikoyan MiG-21STM (Fishbed-K) cutaway drawing key

1 Pitot tube
2 Roll sensor
3 Radome
4 Radar antenna
5 Air intake
6 IFF antennas
7 Angle of attack sensor
8 R2L (High Fix) fire control
9 Nosewheel housing
10 BLC device
11 Avionics
12 ADC intake
13 Avionics
14 Nosewheel retraction actuator
15 Nosewheel leg
16 Nosewheel door
17 Nosewheel fork
18 Nosewheel
19 Rudder pedals
20 Control stick
21 Radar display and instrument panel
22 Windshield
23 Rearview mirror
24 Cockpit canopy
25 Throttle
26 FOD deflector
27 Auxiliary air intake
28 Ejection seat rails
29 Ejection seat gears
30 K-13A (Atoll) missile
31 Missile launching shoe
32 Advanced Atoll missile
33 Missile launching shoe
34 Fuel (T-6) tank
35 Starboard navigation light (blue-green)
36 Radioaltimetre dielectric
37 Wing fence
38 Static discharger
39 KM-1 «zero-zero» ejection seat
40 Multi-spar wing construction
41 Aileron
42 Flap actuator fairing
43 Fuel (T-6) tank
44 Starboard mainwheel leg
45 RSIU (Markham) transmitter (data link) and air-conditioning system
46 Air intake
47 Fuel tank (MiG-21SMT only)
48 Actuators
49 Control runs
50 Fin leading edge construction
51 Fin construction
52 Anti-flutter balance horn
53 Starboard all-moving tailplane
54 Rudder actuator
55 VHF/UHF dielectric
56 IFF antennas
57 Tail navigation light (white)
58 Rudder
59 Rudder construction
60 Brake-chute bullet fairing
61 Brake-chute
62 Variable geometry nozzle
63 Tail warning radar
64 Air scoop
65 Actuator fairing
66 Tailplane pivot
67 Tailplane construction
68 Tailplane skin
69 Anti-flutter balance horn
70 Static discharger
71 Afterburner
72 Afterburner cooling intake
73 Ventral fin
74 Tumansky R-13 turbojet engine

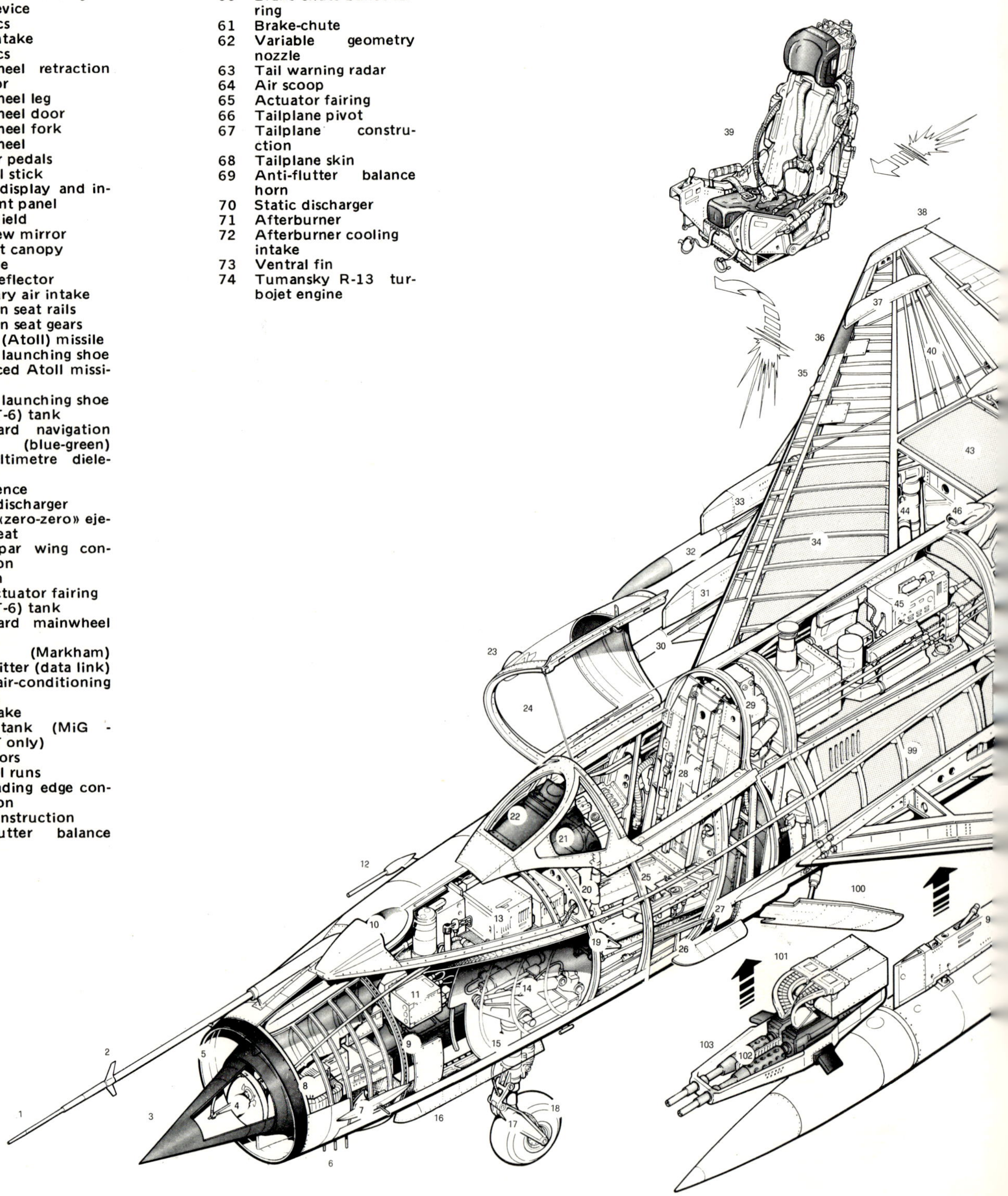

75 Flap
76 Aileron
77 Static discharger
78 Wingtip
79 Radioaltimetre dipole
80 Wing fence
81 Radioaltimetre dielectric
82 Port navigation light (red)
83 Multispar wing construction
84 Fuel (T-6) tank
85 Flap actuator fairing
86 Port mainwheel leg
87 Missile launching shoe
88 Port mainwheel and brake
89 Missile launching shoe
90 Advanced Atoll missile
91 Pylon
92 UV-16-57 55 mm rocketlauncher

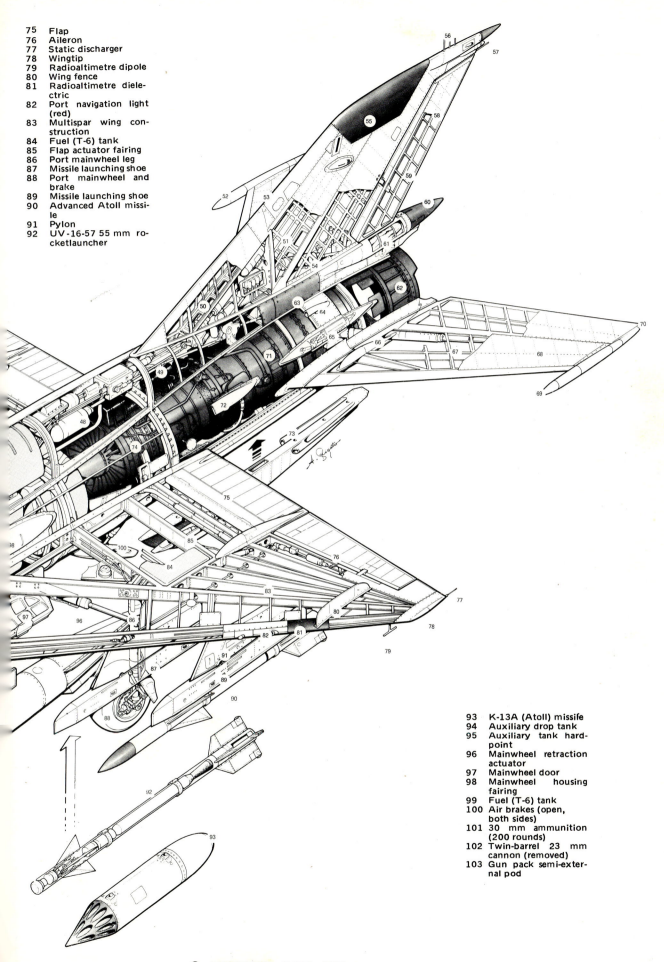

93 K-13A (Atoll) missile
94 Auxiliary drop tank
95 Auxiliary tank hardpoint
96 Mainwheel retraction actuator
97 Mainwheel door
98 Mainwheel housing fairing
99 Fuel (T-6) tank
100 Air brakes (open, both sides)
101 30 mm ammunition (200 rounds)
102 Twin-barrel 23 mm cannon (removed)
103 Gun pack semi-external pod

Soviet airman checks a VU-57B rocket launcher under the wing of a MiG-21.

The built-in armament vary according to the different models, while those of the missile load are principally composed 2-4 air-to-air K-13A (AA-2 Atoll) missiles. Three or five hardpoints for external loads exist to which it is possible to apply, besides air-air missiles, 490 litre auxiliary drop tanks, 500 kg M-62 delay-fuze bombs, 57 mm UV-16-57 or VU-57B rocket-launchers for unguided rockets and 130 mm S-24 air-to-surface rockets in addition to similar major calibre (220 and 325 mm) types.
The following models have been built in mass-production:

MiG-21F (Fishbed-B): (F stands for «Forsirovanny», boosted engine), this version is equipped with a 5,750 kg/s RD-11F turbojet substituting the previous 5,100 kg/s RD-11 one. Its production began in late 1957 and it was delivered to the V-VS in October 1959. The MiG-21F was not equipped with a 30 mm NR-30 right cannon to economize on weight and space.
MiG-21F (Fishbed-C): during mass production the MiG-21F's fin chord was enlarged and the leading edge design was changed. The aircraft made its first appearance at the 1961 Tushino Air Show. It was also distinguishable for its dorsal fairing which allowed the internal fuel capacity to increase from 2,340 to 2,850 litres. Czechoslovakia also began producing this model at the beginning of the 1960's; however, the Czech version was somewhat different in that in lacked posterior transparents in the cockpit. The project is designated as E-66.
MiG-21PF (Fishbed-D): (PF stands for «Perekhvatchik Forsirovanny», boosted interceptor), it was shown for the first time at Tushino in 1961 and marked the appearance of a limited all-weather capacity aircraft. The aircraft presented a shifted nose probe, a fire control with an R2L (High Fix-B) radar contained in a more protruding conical radome, cannon fairings removed, replanning of the cockpit posterior and alterations in the landing gear. The final version, which followed the aerodynamic test-bed presented at Tushino, adopted a fin with an enlarged chord as standard. Subsequently, other detailed changes

were made on the MiG-21PF: the adoption of a new lodging for the brake-chute, alterations on the ventral fin and installation of the SPS (Sduva Pogranichnovo Sloya) system for Boundary Layer Control (BLC) on flaps, as well as, assisted take-off rocket attachments. This variation is also known as MiG-21SPS or MiG-21PF (SPS). The export version MiG-21FL (Forsirovanny Lokator, strenghtened by search radar) lacked these last two features; E-77 or MiG-21PF-77 was the project designation. The name Fishbed-E was mistakenly assigned to the sub-version MiG-21F-13 of the Fishbed-C. Beginning with the 1974 models, the MiG-21PF adopted a fin with a straight leading edge and was predisposed for eventual installation of a GP-9 pod with a 23mm Gsh-23 twin mount in the belly.
MiG-21PFM (Fishbed-F): (Perekhvatchik Forsirovanny Modifikatsirovanny, the same modification), practically speaking, this is the final version of the above with a new type of ejection seat and canopy with separate windscreen and hood fastened on the right. It is known as Type 77 in India.
MiG-21PFM Analog: this model was equipped with a delta composite wing having the same wing planform as that of the Tupolev Tu-144 (Charger) and used as aerodynamic test-bed.

The flying suit of a Soviet pilot in front of an old MiG-21F (Fishbed-C).

The tactical STOL version of the MiG-21PFM (Fishbed-G) did not proceed beyond the prototype stage.

MiG-21PFM (Fishbed-G): this was an experimental STOL prototype with two vertical lift jets inserted in the middle of the fuselage to shorten the take-off run. It had no follow up.

MiG- 21PFMA (Fishbed-J): (also known as MiG-21M or-21PM) it is characterized by the long dorsal fairing and by two ulterior hardpoints for external loads (which therefore pass from three to five). The motor is a 6,200 kg/s R-11-F2S-300 turbojet. It features the KM-1 «zero-zero» ejection seat. In India it is known as the MiG-21M or Type 88 and has fixed armings made up of two 23mm Gsh-23 cannons.

MiG-21R (Fishbed-H): this multi-sensor recon- naissance and ECM (Electronic Counter-Measures) version of the MiG-21PFMA is characterized by a dorsal dielectric, ECM fairings at the wing tips and ventral pod with reconnaissance apparatus.

MiG-21MF (Fishbed-J): sometimes called Fishbed-J Mk.2 by the press, it was completed in 1971; it has a 6,600 kg/s R-13 or R-13-300 turbojet, retroscope mirror, protective strakes on the supplementary air intakes and a two barrel system 23mm Gsh-23 with 100 rounds per barrel.

MiG-21RF (Fishbed-H): reconnaissance version of the above.

MiG-21SMT (Fishbed-K): it is identical to the MiG-21MF except for the addition of a new type of posterior alarm radar which warns the pilot when the aircraft is exposed to missile attack.

MiG-21U (Mongol-A): (Utebenny, training), a two-seat training version, also known as the MiG-21UTI or Type 66-400 in India.

MiG-21U (Mongol-B): this variation is, apparently, identical to the above except for the appearance of a broad chord fin (known in India as Type 66-600).

A flight of MiG-21MF (Fishbed-J) made a good will visit to France some years ago. Photograph was taken in Reims.

MiG-21US (SPS) (Mongol-C): a variation of the above with a retroscope system (including a retractable periscope) and SPS wings.

MiG-21UM (Mongol-D): a training version with R-13-300 engine, SPS and four wing hardpoints.

Shenyang F-8 (Fishbed-C): a Chinese copy of the MiG-21F.

MiG-21MF (Fishbed-L): externally recognizable because the auxiliary air intakes lack protection strakes; it is provided with a tactic navigation system similar to the TACAN.

MiG-21 bis (Fishbed-L/M): this is a «reengined» MiG-21MF with the new 7,500 kg/s R-25 Tumansky turbojet.

Inspite of the MiG-21's modest combat radius, which reduces its possibilities as an interceptor and limits its capacity of ground attack, it has hag great sales success and it is still in service in many countries. Algeria has two groups approximately totaling 35 in service, Afghanistan has between 38-40, Albania has 12 F-8s, a certain number of models have been used by Angola in the recent War of Independence (but it is not known if they are still in service), Bangladesh has 11 MiG-21s, Bulgaria employs four groups with 48, Czechoslovakia has 22 groups with 320, 80 of which are reconnaissance, the number used by the Chinese is uncertain (possibly 40), North Korea 12 groups with 150, Cuba three groups with 50, Egypt 230-250, Finland 41, six of which are used for training, East Germany 18 groups with 294, India ten groups with 220 (plus an additional stock of 126), Indonesia 15 (none of which are presently operative), Iraq five groups with 100, Israel one (wartime prey), Yugoslåvia eight groups with 110, Poland 28 groups with 400, 48 of these are reconnaissance, Rumania 80 plus a few used

Line-up of MiG-21SMTs (Fishbed-K).

The MiG-21SMT (Fishbed-K) is probably the MiG-21MF refitted with a new passive warning radar and provision for the Advanced Atoll missiles.

for training, Syria approximately 250, Somalia one group with 24, Sudan one group with 18, Uganda one group, Hungary seven groups with 80, the USSR with 1,700 of the most recent MiG-21 models, Viet-Nam four groups with approximately 70, South Yemen one group of 12. The figures on the production of the MiG-21 vary (some go as far as to suggest tens of thousands), however, without a doubt, the number produced is not under 5,000.

Mikoyan MiG-21MF (Fishbed-J)
All-weather air superiority fighter, single seat

Power plant: One 51,03 kN (5.200 kg/st, 11,465 lb st) dry and 64,77 kN (6.600 kg/st, 14,550 lb/st) Tumansky R-13-300 (SPS) axial turbojet. Fuel capacity: 2.640 l (580 gal) internally and 1.470 l (323 gal) internally.

Dimensions: wing span 7,15 m (23.45 ft); length 15,76 m (51.70 ft); length without nose probe 13,98 m (45.86 ft); height 4,55 m (14,93 ft); wing area 23,0 sq m (247.57 sq ft); undercarriage track 2,69 m (8.82 ft).

Weights: Loaded (without external loads) 7.900 kg (17,415 lb); maximum take-off 9.400 kg (20,725 lb).

Performance: Maximum speed 2.230 km/h (1,385 mph) at 11.000 m (36,089 ft) (Mach 2.1), 1.300 km/h (808 mph) at sea level (Mach 1.06); landing speed 270 km/h (178 mph); service ceiling 18.000 m (59,050 ft); range 1.100 km (683 mls); ferry range 1.790 km (1,112 mls).

Armament: One twin-barrel 23-mm Gsh-23 cannon with 200 rounds and 1.500 kg (3,300 lb) warload.

MiG-21PFM (Fishbed-F), IAP-VO (Strany), Soviet V-V, Moscow Military District, July 1967. The aircraft belongs to the aerobatic team previously mounted on MiG-19.

Sukhoi Interceptors

Su-9 and Su-11 (Fishpot)

The Sukhoi Su-9 (Fishpot) came to life because of a requirement issued by the V-VS in 1953 for a single seat, all-weather interceptor fighter. The design, presented by the Pavel Osipovich Sukhoi Engineering Staff (recently rehabilitated after several years of political «mishap»), was derived from that of the Su-7 tactical aircraft and this design clashed with the ones presented by Mikoyan: the I-75F, E-152 and its derivative (known as the E-153 in the West). The Sukhoi, equipped with delta wing, was named T-405 and it won out against the Mikoyan models, even if they presented more advanced features, because it offered a great interchangeability of parts with the Su-7.

Two prototypes were constructed from this project. The first one was piloted for the first time by Vladimir Ilyushin at Ramenskoye at the beginning of 1956. It featured a «type F-86D» fire control antenna system and was armed with a 30mm cannon on the right wing root. It was called Su-9 (Fishpot-A). Instead, the second prototype (Fishpot-B) had the same radome air intake complex as the Su-7. Both prototypes took part in the Tushino Air Show on June 14, 1956. The Su-9 (Fishpot-B), armed with four

AA-1 Alkali radar guided missiles, was selected as the mass-production model. The aircraft began distribution to the air interception units of the IAP-VO Strany, starting with the air districts of Moscow and Baku, in 1959.

The Sukhoi Su-9 Fishpot-B is an all-weather interceptor fighter principally used for local air defense, that is, protection of the major densely populated areas and of the most important military installations. The propulsive system is made up of an axial flow Lyulka AL-7F turbojet. The engine has a two-stage compressor, a compression rate of 8:1 and a specific fuel consumption of 0.817 kg/kgs/h dry and 2.2 kg/kgs/h with afterburner on maximum. The fire control is an R1L (High Fix-A) in S-band with an approximate range of 19 km (12mls) and the avionics is similar to that of the MiG-21 but slightly more complete and advanced. The delta wing is characterized by a 57° swept at the leading edge, clipped wingtips and a trailing edge with an extremely light negative swept. The armings consist of four suspended AA-1 Alkali missiles with four hardpoints which also carry the command transmission. Two ventral hardpoints can hold up two 600 litre (132 gal) auxiliary drop tanks.

A ready-to-scramble flight of Su-9 (Fishpot-B) interceptor fighters.

Sukhoi Su-11 (Fishpot-C)
All-weather interceptor fighter, single seat

Power plant: One 68,69 kN (7,000 kg/st., 15,430 lb/st) dry and 107,95 kN (11.000 kg/s, 24,250 lb/st) reheat Lyulka AL-7F-1 axial turbojet.

Dimensions: Wing span 9,50 m (31.18 ft); length (with nose probe) 18,90 m (62 ft), (without nose probe) 18,10 m (59.38 ft); height 5,12 m (16.80 ft); wing area 39.50 sq m (425 sq ft); undercarriage track 4,00 m (13.12 ft).

Weights: Empty 9.100 kg (20,060 lb); loaded 12.300 kg (27,115 lb); maximum take-off 14.000 kg (30,865 lb).

Performance: Maximum speed 1.890 km/h (1,174 mph) at 12.000 m (39,300 ft) (Mach 1.78), 1.160 km/h (721 mph) at 300 m (1,000 ft) (Mach 0.95) «clean», 1.270 km/h (789 mph) at 12.000 m (39,300 ft) (Mach 1.19) with two AAM and two external tanks; initial climb rate 137-152 m/sec (26,970-29,900 ft/min); service ceiling 21.150 m (69,400 ft); absolute ceiling 28.500 m (93,500 ft); maximum combat radius 460 km (286 mls); range 1.100 km (685 mls).

Armament: two AA-3 Anab-R (radar) and - IR (infrared) air-to-air missiles.

Sukhoi Su-9 (Fishpot-B) cutaway drawing key

1 Nose probe
2 Attitude sensors
3 Radome
4 Radar antenna
5 Air intake
6 R1L fire control
7 Attitude sensors wiring
8 Windshield
9 Instrument panel
10 Radar display
11 Cockpit canopy (rearward opening)
12 Canopy demist
13 Right console
14 Ejection seat
15 Headrest
16 COM system
17 K-5 (Alkali) air-to-air missile
18 K-5 command antenna
19 Missile pylon
20 Fuel tank
21 Leading edge
22 Fuel tank
23 Wing skin
24 Static discharger
25 Aileron
26 Flap
27 Airbrake
28 Tailplanes control runs
29 Fin
30 Leading edge construction

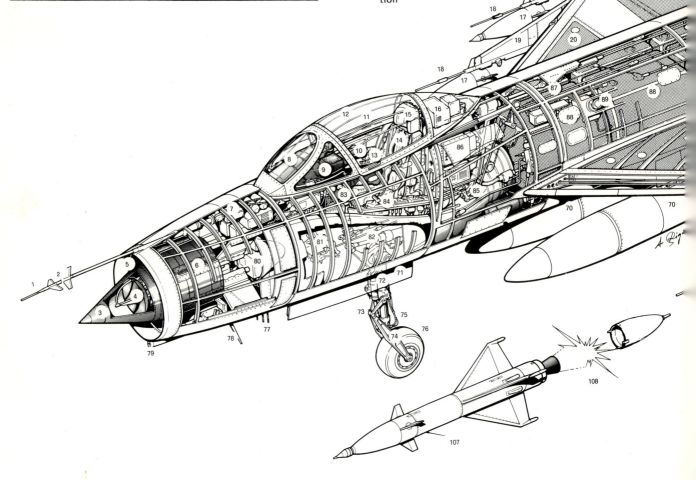

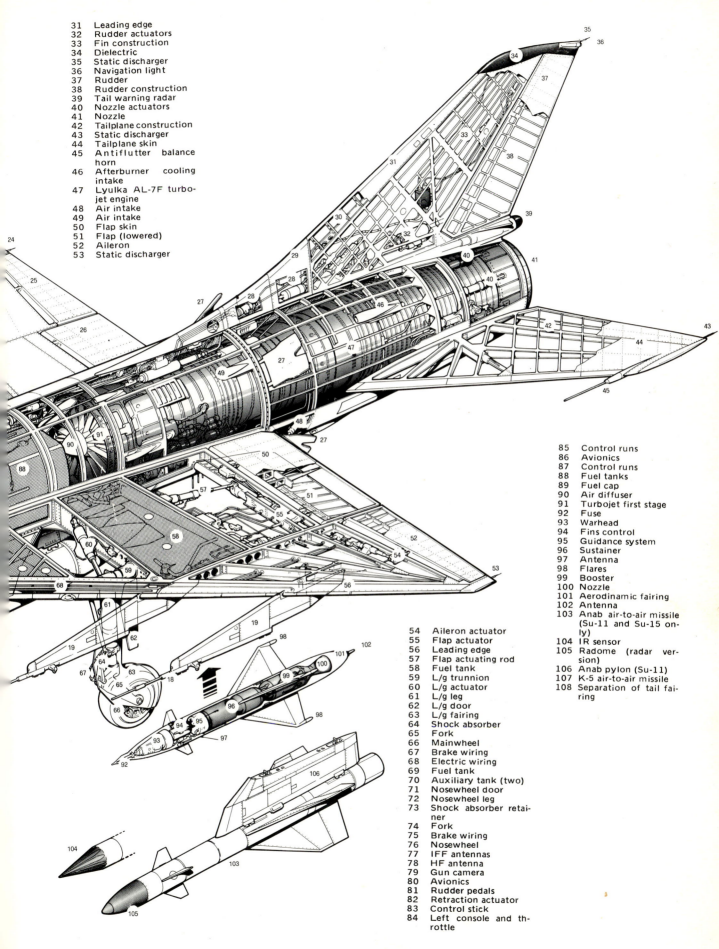

31 Leading edge
32 Rudder actuators
33 Fin construction
34 Dielectric
35 Static discharger
36 Navigation light
37 Rudder
38 Rudder construction
39 Tail warning radar
40 Nozzle actuators
41 Nozzle
42 Tailplane construction
43 Static discharger
44 Tailplane skin
45 Antiflutter balance horn
46 Afterburner cooling intake
47 Lyulka AL-7F turbojet engine
48 Air intake
49 Air intake
50 Flap skin
51 Flap (lowered)
52 Aileron
53 Static discharger

54 Aileron actuator
55 Flap actuator
56 Leading edge
57 Flap actuating rod
58 Fuel tank
59 L/g trunnion
60 L/g actuator
61 L/g leg
62 L/g door
63 L/g fairing
64 Shock absorber
65 Fork
66 Mainwheel
67 Brake wiring
68 Electric wiring
69 Fuel tank
70 Auxiliary tank (two)
71 Nosewheel door
72 Nosewheel leg
73 Shock absorber retainer
74 Fork
75 Brake wiring
76 Nosewheel
77 IFF antennas
78 HF antenna
79 Gun camera
80 Avionics
81 Rudder pedals
82 Retraction actuator
83 Control stick
84 Left console and throttle

85 Control runs
86 Avionics
87 Control runs
88 Fuel tanks
89 Fuel cap
90 Air diffuser
91 Turbojet first stage
92 Fuse
93 Warhead
94 Fins control
95 Guidance system
96 Sustainer
97 Antenna
98 Flares
99 Booster
100 Nozzle
101 Aerodinamic fairing
102 Antenna
103 Anab air-to-air missile (Su-11 and Su-15 only)
104 IR sensor
105 Radome (radar version)
106 Anab pylon (Su-11)
107 K-5 air-to-air missile
108 Separation of tail fairing

Sukhoi Su-9 (Fishpot-B) IAP-VO (Strany), Soviet V-VS, Moscow Military District, 1961-66.

Sukhoi Su-11 (Fishpot-C) IAP-VO (Strany), Soviet V-VS, Moscow-Domodedovo, July 1967.

Sukhoi Su-15 (Flagon-A) Soviet V-VS, Ramenskoye (near Moscow), prototype of the test pilot Vladimir Ilyushin, 1964-67. According to unchecked sources a whole unit had overall black Flagons.

Sukhoi Su-15 (Flagon-A) IAP-VO (Strany), Soviet V-VS, Moscow Military District, July 1967; aircraft with such livery are said to belong to the **Golden Hawks** unit. Later a Flagon-mounted aerobatic team appeared with aircraft sporting an overall red finish with natural metal undersurfaces.

Sukhoi Su-15 (Flagon-A) IAP-VO (Strany), Soviet V-VS, unknown unit, 1975; it is a late production Flagon-A with larger tail warning radar atop the rudder.

The aircraft armament had already proven themselves rather insufficient when they entered service, so much so that, in order to increase their power, Sukhoi's engineering staff had to develop a new version of the aircraft which was accepted in service as the Su-11; besides being at least one metre longer than the Su-9, it principally differed in the armings, which consisted of an AA-3 Anab-R missile and an AA-6 Anab-IR one (the former with guided radar and the latter with infrared) transported suspending from the wing pylons. At the same time a 100 kw fire control with an approximate 30 km (18 miles) range was mounted. This adjustment, together with the adoption of an AL-7F-1 turbojet which proved to give a better performance, also required an air intake with bigger diametre.

The Su-9 also gave life to a training tandem two-seat version called Su-9U (Maiden).

On July 14, 1959 the Su-9 reached a record climb altitude of 28,520 m with pilot Vladimir Ilyushin at the commands and on September 4, 1962 the Su-11 reached an altitude sustained flight record climbing to 21,170 m on a circuit of 15/25 km. The number of Su-9s and Su-11s built is unknown, but approximately 300 Su-11s appeared to be in service in fighter aviation units of the IAP-VO Strany (Air Defence Command) with local defense duties in 1976, while about one hundred Su-9s were adopted by the flight training units.

Neither the Su-9s nor the Su-11s have ever been furnished to foreign Air Forces.

Su-15 (Flagon)

The Sukhoi Su-15 came into being between 1959 and 1962 to fulfill a new specific request put out by the V-VS which asked for a single-seat all-weather interceptor fighter with a maximum velocity that would be superior to any potential opponent. Both Sukhoi and Mikoyan replied, the former presenting his project which derived from the Su-11 and the latter with the E-166. Sukhoi again won the competition and his interceptor (created between 1959 and 1962 and probably called T-431) was taken over by the V-VS as the Su-15 (Flagon). The first prototype was test-piloted by Vladimir Ilyushin, probably, in 1964. No news of the Su-15's existence leaked out until July 7, 1967 when the prototype, several mass production examples and a STOL version were presented at Domodedovo (Moscow).

It is clearly evident that the Sukhoi Su-15 was taken from the Su-9/11 series, even though the engine has been radically changed and it is classified as an all-weather interceptor fighter.

The engine consists of two Lyulka AL-21 F-3 axial flow turbojets. A large radome with side air intakes, in which is contained a Skip Spin fire control with a large diameter antenna, is found in the nose (forward fuselage). The firing radar is a modern pulse type and it operates in X-band (3.3cm) with a pulse repeat frequency between 2,700 and 3,000 pulses/sec. which last for 0.5 mi-

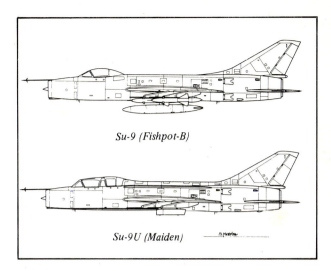

Su-9 (Fishpot-B)

Su-9U (Maiden)

Above: the Su-11 (Fishpot-C) with two Anab AAM missiles. Below: the previous version (Su-9 Fishpot-B) with pylons for four older Alkali AAM.

crosec. It has approximately 100 kw of power and a range of 40 km (25 mls) and in favourable conditions it can reach up to 60 km, (37 mls). The pilot seat is protected by a sliding back canopy with rear armour and it is equipped with a «zero height» ejection seat.

The arming is composed of two air-air AA-3 Anab-R or IR missiles, while the most recent models seem to adapt themselves to the semi-external installation of a two barrel 23 mm Gsh-23 cannon. The fuel capacity is increased by the addition of two 600 litre (132 gal.) ventral tanks. The prototype and the first version of the Flagon-A series gave way to the experimental version

Clockwise: the Sukhoi Su-15 (Flagon-A) Mach 2 + class all-weather interceptor. One of the first Flagon prototypes was this all-black aircraft coded «47». A later produced Flagon-A had a bigger tail warning radar above the rudder. Below: an aerobatic team of three Flagon-A trailing coloured smoke.

of the STOL Flagon-B fighter-bomber. This version was equipped with three lift engines installed in the fuselage and the composite delta wing planform had a greater span, a variation which had no further development. Instead the Sukhoi Su-15U Flagon-C tandem two-seat trainers were mass produced along with the Flagon-D and Flagon-E versions. The latter have just recently been put into service and they should differentiate themselves from the Flagon-As in their wing design (similar to the Flagon-B) and the possibility of employing air-air AA-6-2 Acrid (ex-Advanced Anab) missiles which have a greater thrust than the preceeding AA-3 Anab missiles.

The aircraft entered service in 1967 and at first were only made available to experimental units and one or two aerobatic teams. The units began receiving large quantities between 1969 and 1970 and this seems to have continued in the years following. At present, in the V-VS, the Flagon-A, -C, -D, and -Es furnish from 11 to 20 regiments of the IAP-VO Strany, the Fighter Command of the Air Forces, with approximately 625 to 935 single-seat and 75 to 235 two-seat aircraft. This

aircraft continually remained in mass production (15 pieces a month in 1971 according to American figures) at least until 1975 continuing to substitute the Su-9s, Su-15s of the first series and the Yak-28Ps and they seem destined to remain in first line service well beyond 1980.

Sukhoi Su-15 (Flagon-A)
All-weather interceptor fighter, single-seat

Power plant: Two 76,54 kN (7.800 kg/st, 17,195 lb/st) dry and 109,91 kN (11.200 kg/s, 24,690 lb/st) reheat Lyulka AL-21F-3 axial turbojets.

Dimensions: (extimated) wing span 9,38 m (30.77 ft); length 20,00 m (65.61 ft), (without noseprobe) 18,30 m (60.04 ft); height 4,83 m (15.84 ft); wing area 39 mq (419.80 sq. ft); undercarriage track 4,80 m (15.75 ft).

Weights: (extimated) loaded 7.250 kg (16,000 lb); maximum take-off 18.600 kg (41,000 lb).

Performance: (extimated) maximum speed 2,654 km/h (1,649 mph) at 12.000 m (39,300 ft) (Mach 2.5), 1.464 km/h (909 mph) at 300 m (1,000 ft) (Mach 1.2); service ceiling 19.000 m (62,300 ft); combat radius 725 km (450 mls); range 2.400 km (1,490 mls).

Armament: two AA-3 Anab-R or -IR air-to-air missiles.

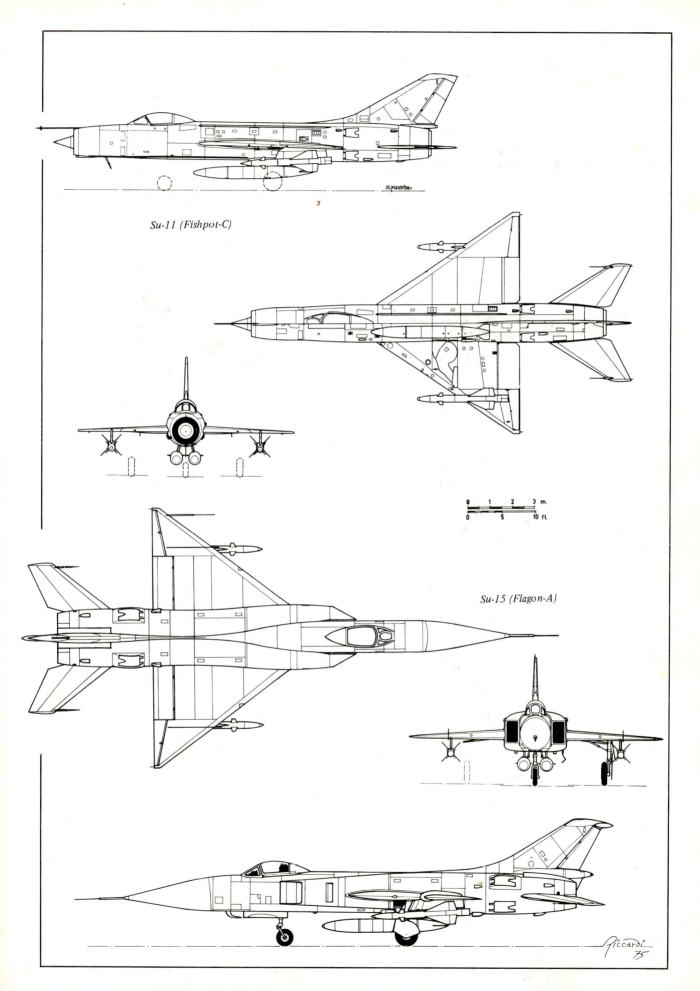

Su-11 (Fishpot-C)

Su-15 (Flagon-A)

0 1 2 3 m.
0   5   10 ft.

Sukhoi Su-7 (Fitter)

Nice shot of a Sukhoi Su-7MF (Fitter-A). In the background are MiG-21s, MiG-19s and MiG-17s.

In 1953 the V-VS issued a new series of specifications asking for a tactical close support aircraft highly supersonic in horizontal flight. According to common Soviet practice this aerodynamics investigation was carried out by the TSAGI (Tsentralnii AeroGidrodinamiceskii Institut, Central Institute of Aerodynamics). Pavel Osipovich Sukhoi's engineering staff presented a project which competed against one presented by Mikoyan, the E-2A (Faceplate): the former was chosen.

The Su-7 was flown for the first time in late 1955 and it was presented to the public at the Tushino Air Show of June 24, 1956. In the years that followed its evolution continued through the pre-series aircraft and in 1959 the aircraft was ordered into service, with the V-VS Tactical Air Force Command, as the Su-7B (B stands for Bombardirovschik, bombardment). This was verified when, in the summer of 1961, 21 Su-7Bs

paraded in the Tushino Air Show. The ASCC assigned the code name Fitter to this aircraft. The first production version differed slightly from earlier versions. The most noteworthy modifica-

A Su-7B (Fitter-A) close support aircraft with the usual pair of 600 litres drop tanks and two practice bombs.

A Su-7MF (fitted with RATOG «bottles») touching down at the historical Domodedovo air show in 1967.

tions were the adoption of wiring in the external fairings and shifting of the nose probe from the top to the right side of the air intake.

In 1961 the Su-7Bs began replacing the older models.

In May 1965 several pre-series Su-7s took part in the first «near operational» mission carrying out intimidating flights over West Berlin.

The Su-7 again came into the limelight during the Six Day War when the Egyptian Air Force was able to put 30 examples into service; however, 14 of these were destroyed on the ground and 6 in air combat at the end of the conflict. The Egyptian Su-7s took part in several clashes during the period of tension, in the Mediterranean area, which followed the 1967 conflict; an episode worthy of mention occured on April 19, 1971 when an Egyptian Su-7 was shot down by an Israeli Raytheon MIM-23A Hawk missile (the first aircraft to be shot down in action by a missile of this type).

The Su-7 was again called on to perform a difficult task in the subcontinent of India in December 1971. When the war between India and

The tandem two-seat conversion training is the Su-7U (Moujik).

Pakistan broke out India had 145 Sukhoi Su-7s in its Air Force, only 95 of which were combat ready; after ten days of combat only slightly more than 60 were still in service! Thirty-one Su-7s were definitely proven destroyed and three probably shot down; six or seven Indian fighter-bombers were shot down by the Pakistani anti-aircraft artillery and nine or ten by small arms fire; one Su-7 was shot down by an F-104A Starfighter, five by North American Sabres six to eight by Shenyang F-6S (Farmer-C) and two or three by Mirage IIIs, one of which was shot down by means of a MATRA R.530 air-to-air missile.

Even though the aircraft did not demonstrate any particularly interesting features, it is believed that its production was prolonged until at least the end of 1973. The Su-7 was again called on to fight in the «Yom Kippur» War of October 6, 1973. Immediately before this conflict the Egyptian and Syrian Air Forces had received new material: Egypt drew up 120 Su-7s and Syria set up 30. At the end of the conflict Egypt lost approximately 65 fighters while it is too difficult to determine the Syrian figures which refer to a specific type of aircraft; however the figure of 80 MiG-21s and Su-7s seems to be a reliable estimate. Besides the production of prototypes and pre-series models previously mentioned, the Su-7s were also developed in the versions listed below. Since the NATO code nicknames were not differentiated, the Western press has resorted to «Mark» in order to identify the following changes.

Su-7B (Fitter-A) Mk.2: first version to be mass-produced for the V-VS; the differences have already been described in the text.

Su-7U (Moujik): a two-seat training version which features a different cockpit with a slightly raised instructor's seat. It was officially presented at Moscow-Domodedovo in August 1967.

Su-7BM (Fitter-A) Mk.2A: this version produced by permission in Czechoslovakia is practically

Sukhoi Su-7BMK (Fitter-A) cutaway drawing key

1 Attitude sensors
2 Nose probe
3 Air intake
4 Radar antenna
5 SRD-5M (High Fix) radar
6 Avionics
7 Auxiliary air intakes
8 Control stick
9 Instrument panel
10 Windshield (with de-icing system)
11 HUDsight
12 Cockpit canopy
13 Rearview mirror
14 Headrest
15 Ejection seat
16 Left console and throttle
17 Air intake trunking
18 Avionics
19 COM system
20 Air-conditioning system
21 Control runs
22 Wire runs
23 Wing leading edge
24 Fuel tanks
25 30 mm ammunition
26 Wire fairings
27 Fuel tanks
28 Pitot tube
29 Wing construction
30 Air diffuser
31 APU air intake
32 Lyulka AL-7F-1 turbojet engine
33 Wire fairings
34 Airbrake (open)
35 Oil tank
36 Oil cooling air intake
37 Airbrake (open)
38 Rudder actuator
39 Actuators controls
40 Fin construction
41 Dielectric
42 Static discharger and navigation light

43 Tail warning radar
44 Rudder
45 Brake chute housing doors
46 Twin brake chute
47 Nozzle
48 Afterburner cooling intake
49 Afterburner
50 Tailplane actuator
51 Tailplane construction
52 Static discharger
53 Antiflutter balance horn
54 Tailplane pivot
55 Airbrake (open)
56 Engine gearbox
57 Assisted take-off rocket
58 Flap
59 Aileron
60 Static discharger
61 Wing fence
62 Navigation light
63 Pitot tube
64 Leading edge
65 Aileron actuator
66 Rocket launcher
67 Wing fence
68 Flap actuator
69 Hardpoint
70 Port landing gear
71 L/g door
72 Fork and shock absorber
73 L/g pivot
74 Rear main spar
75 L/g actuating jack
76 Mainwheel housing
77 Front main spar
78 Nudelmann-Richter NR-30 30 mm cannon
79 Leading edge construction

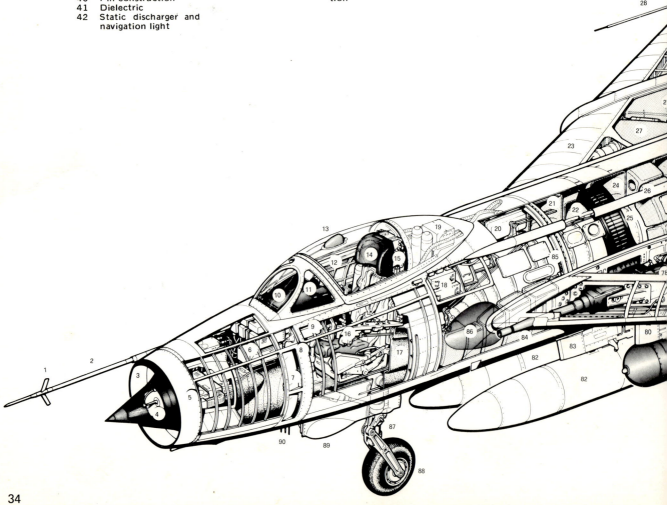

34

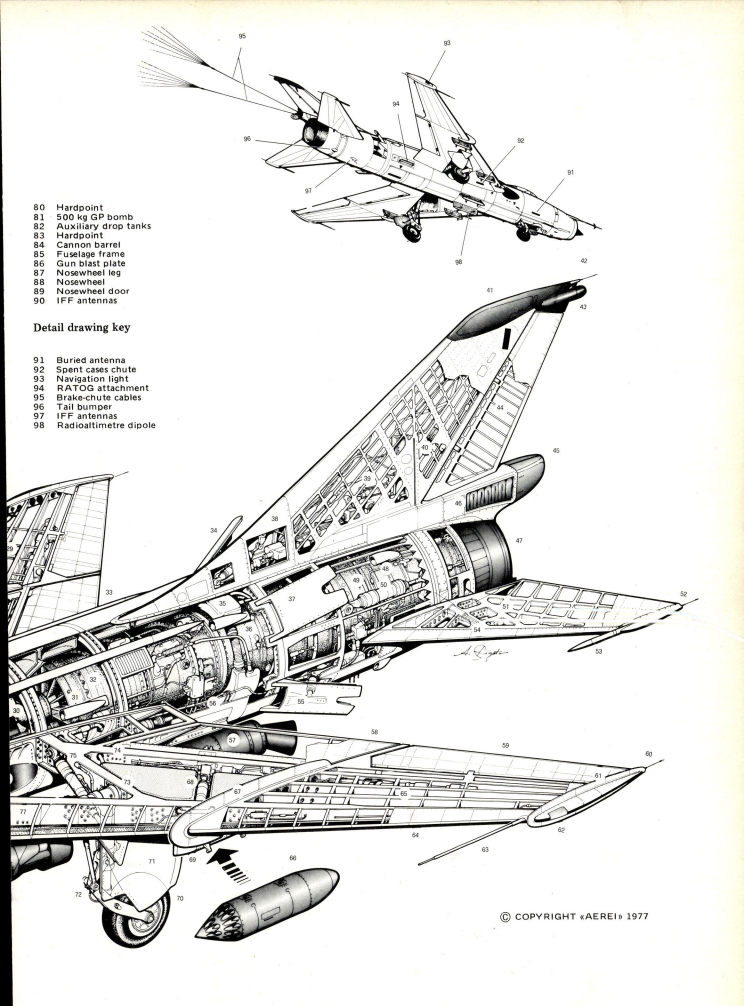

80 Hardpoint
81 500 kg GP bomb
82 Auxiliary drop tanks
83 Hardpoint
84 Cannon barrel
85 Fuselage frame
86 Gun blast plate
87 Nosewheel leg
88 Nosewheel
89 Nosewheel door
90 IFF antennas

Detail drawing key

91 Buried antenna
92 Spent cases chute
93 Navigation light
94 RATOG attachment
95 Brake-chute cables
96 Tail bumper
97 IFF antennas
98 Radioaltimetre dipole

35

Soviet colour photographs are often of poor quality. Above: a Su-7U operational trainer during an assisted take-off. Below: a Su-7BMK fires a salvo of S-5MK antitank unguided rockets during an exercise.

identical to the Su-7B.

Su-7BKL (Fitter-A) Mk.3: a version of the above also built in Czechoslovakia with a strengthened landing gear, larger diameter nosewheel, attachments for assisted take-off rockets, a double parachute brake, here placed at the base of the fin, able to take-off from short and semiprepared runways.

Su-7MF (Fitter-A) Mk.3A: the Soviet version of the Su-7BKL featuring a Lyulka AL-7F-1 turbojet with thrust increased from 10,000 to 11,000 kg. It was presented in the summer of 1967.

Su-7BMK (Fitter-A) Mk.4: this version was presented in the summer of 1972; it was characterized by two new external wing hardpoints.

Su-7BMK (Fitter-A) Mk.4A: identical to the above, identifiable by a retroscope which is on the ceiling of the canopy. The first prototype of this aircraft appeared in the summer of 1973.

The Su-7 has been widely diffused and it is in service in the following countries (the number of aircraft in service are in parenthesis): the USSR (400 to 500), Czechoslovakia (75), Cuba (40), Egypt (108), Syria (approximately 50), East Germany (approximately 160), Hungary (40), India (161), Poland (60), Viet-Nam (the actual number has not been confirmed), Afghanistan (14), North Korea (28), Israel (one, war prey), Iraq (50). A total of 1,600 to 1,800 examples have been produced.

Sukhoi Su-7BMK (Fitter-A) Mk.4/4A
Clear weather fighter-bomber with limited all-weather capability, single seat

Power plant: One 68, 69 kN (7.000 kg/st, 15,430 lb/st) dry and 107,95 kN (11.000 kg/s, 24,250 lb/st) reheat Lyulka AL-7F-1 axial turbojet. Fuel capacity: 3.175 kg (7,000 lb) or about 3.980 l (875 gal) internally and 952 kg (2,100 lb) or about 1.195 l (262 gal) externally.

Dimensions: wing span 9,25 m (30.35 ft); length 18,37 m (60.27 ft), (without nose probe) 16,65 m (54.62 ft); height 4,90 m (16.07 ft); wing area 34,5 sq m (371.35 sq ft); undercarriage track 4,00 m (13.12 ft).

Weights: Empty about 8.700 kg (19,200 lb); loaded 12.310 kg (27,138 lb); maximum take-off 14.000 kg (30,865 lb); maximum overload 14.800 kg. (32,630 lb).

Performance: Maximum speed 1.805-1.910 km/h (1,121-1,187 mph) at 12.000 m (39,300 m) (Mach 1.7-1.8), 1.160 km/h (721 mph) at 300 m (1,000 ft) (Mach 0.95); cruise 835 km/h (519 mph) at 12.000 m (39,300 ft) (Mach 0,786); landing speed about 375 km/h (233 mph); initial climb rate 152 m/sec (30,000 ft/min); service ceiling 15.150 m (49,700 ft); absolute ceiling 29.000 m (95.150 ft); combat radius (hi-lo-hi mission) 450 km (279 mls); range 1.450 km (900 mls).

Armament: two forward firing Nudelmann-Richter NR-30 30-mm cannons in the wing roots with 70-73 rounds per gun and six hardpoints for 3.000 kg (6,615 lb) warload (two ventral and two inner wing pylons for 500 kg/1,100 lb each and two outer wing pylons for 250 kg/550 lb each).

Su-7B (Fitter-A) Ceskoslovenské Letectvo
(Czech Air Force)

5018

Su-7U (Moujik) V-VS, USSR

49

Su-7MB (Fitter-A) Indian Air Force
(provisional camouflage during the
last indo-pakistani war)

Su-7BMK (Fitter-A) AREAF (Arab
Republic of Egypt Air Force)

٧٦٦٤

Su-7MF (Fitter-A), V-VS, USSR (to
note the angle of attack of the assisted
take-off and the shock absorber of
main landing gear at maximum
compression)

60

Pietro Mazzardi

37

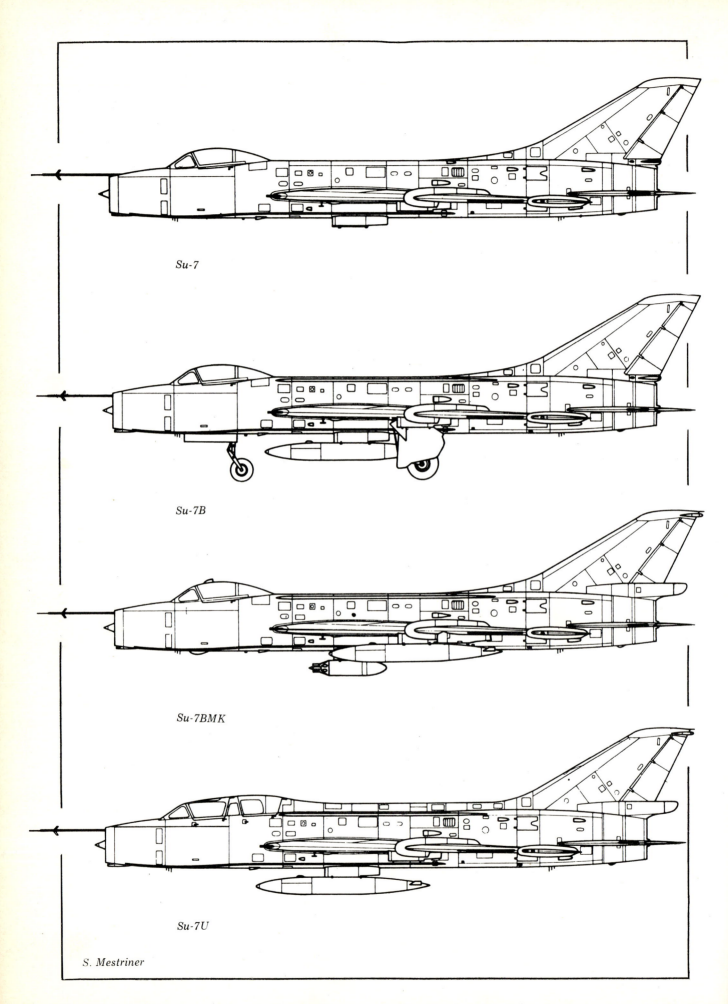

Su-7

Su-7B

Su-7BMK

Su-7U

S. Mestriner

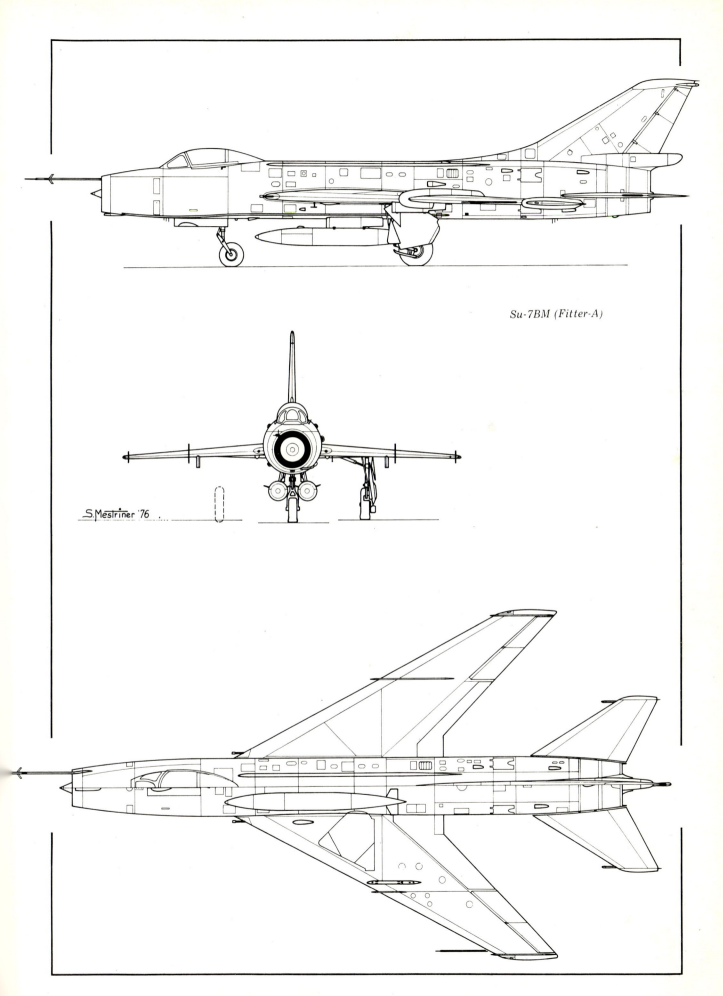

Su-7BM (Fitter-A)

S.Mestriner '76

Sukhoi Su-17/20/22 (Fitter-C)

The Sukhoi Su-20 (a Polish aircraft is depicted above) is the export version of the Su-17 (Fitter-C).

Around 1964-1965 Soviet engineering staffs began to work on different proposals, some entirely new as well as some with partial modifications on existing aircraft, to obviate the deficiencies of the Su-7 (Fitter-A). Sukhoi's staff dedicated itself to one of these proposals and it presented a prototype of a variable geometry aircraft modifying an Su-7B. Also this aircraft, the first Soviet jet with such a wing configuration, appeared in public in the famous Domodedovo Air Show of July 1967. The airframe of the Su-7 did not undergo any changes in this model except for the outer wings which were placed so that they could pass from the original swept to an almost straight one. The landing speed was further reduced thanks to the adoption of a slat on the leading edge.

The first known photograph of a pre-series Su-17 (Fitter-C).

Initially this aircraft was known as Fitter-B in the West and it was no longer heard of until 1972 when the news spread that it would be distributed to the units.

A pre-series version called Su-17 derived from the first prototype which was assigned to an operative testing unit of the FA (Tactical Air Force of the V-VS) and at first it was known as the «improved Fitter-B» in the West. This aircraft distinguished itself from the prototype for the long dorsal spine, meant to increase the fuel capacity, and new avionics. Only in 1974, during an air show in Warsaw, did the series Su-17 make its first public appearance proving that Poland was the first country of the Warsaw Pact, after the USSR, to be equipped with the new fighter-bomber, reclassified in NATO circles as Fitter-C. Su-20 is the name of the version exported to Poland and

The Su-17 prototype (Fitter-B) taking off with wings at minimum swept.

subsequently to other countries while the Fitter-C ordered by Peru is called Su-22.

The Su-17/Su-20 is practically identical, except for small modifications to the landing gear, the ailerons and the flaps, to the Su-7 (Fitter-A). The most important change is caused by the small movement variable geometry wing not only adopted to satisfy range requirements but principally to obtain better take-off and landing performance therefore obviating the deficiencies of the Su-7B. The power plant is composed of a Lyulka AL-21F-3 axial flow turbojet fed by a front air intake and four auxiliary air intakes. It has a 4,625 litre (1,017 gal) fuel capacity contained internally in the fuselage, while two 600 litre (132 gal) auxiliary tanks can be attached to the two external wing hardpoints and probably two others can be suspended on the ventral hardpoints.

The electronic flight equipment is made up of an SRD-5M radar, an SRO-2M IFF, a Sirena 3 tail warning radar, an ASP-5ND gunsight, an ARK-10 radio compass, an RV-UM radioaltimeter, an MRP-56P beacon receiver, an SOD-57M ATC/SIF, a NI-50BM Doppler radar, an SP-50 landing system, an RSBN-2S short range navigation system and R5B-70, RSIU-5, ARL-5 and R-831 radio systems.

The armament consist of two Nudelmann-Richter NR-30 30mm cannons with approximately 70 rounds per gun and a firing rate of 850 rounds per minute, which are located at the wing roots, but sometime not installed, and six or eight hardpoints for external loads. In attack «demolition» missions on hardened hangars and railroads the Fitter-C single-seat all-weather fighter bombers, also destined to substitute the Ilyushin Il-28 (Beagle) light bombers, come armed with 500 kg (1,100

The series production Su-17 has four fuselage hardpoints.

lb) M-62 bombs, while against troop concentration and other «soft» targets 250 kg (550 lb) OFab-250M, 180 kg (400 lb) RBK-250, 250 kg (550 lb) Prosab-250 and other similar types of "cluster bombs" and fragmentation bombs are used. In addition UV-16-57 and VU-57B 16 round rocket launchers and 32 roun UV-32-57 ones containing 57 mm S-5MK anti-tank rockets capable of

Another Polish Su-20. The Fitter-C appears to have limited success as Il-28 replacement.

Sukhoi Su-17 (Fitter-C) cutaway drawing key

1 Pitot tube (dynamic head)
2 Pitch sensors
3 Yaw sensors
4 Sensors to ADC
5 Pitot tube (static head)
6 Radar antenna
7 SRD-5M (Highfix)
8 Avionics
9 Angle of attack sensor
10 Windshield
11 HUDsight
12 Cockpit canopy with demist system
13 Rearview mirror
14 Headrest
15 Ejection seat
16 Auxiliary air intake
17 Instrument panel
18 Control stick
19 Left console and throttle
20 Intake trunking
21 Avionics
22 Air-conditioning and pressure system
23 Antenna
24 Starboard wing
25 Maximum swept position
26 Fuel tanks
27 Control runs
28 30 mm ammunition
29 Air diffuser
30 Tumansky AL-21F-3 turbojet engine
31 Avionics
32 APU intake
33 Airbrake (open)
34 Airbrake (open)
35 Airbrake (open)
36 Tailplane actuator
37 Rudder actuator
38 Fin construction
39 Dielectric
40 Static discharger and navigation light
41 Sirena tail warning radar

42 Twin brake chute
43 Nozzle
44 Tailplane construction
45 Antiflutter balance
46 Static discharger
47 IFF antennas
48 Flap
49 Glove
50 Slot
51 Maximum swept position
52 Aileron
53 Aileron construction
54 Navigation light
55 Wing construction
56 Slat
57 Pylon
58 Wing pivot
59 Wing fence
60 L/g door
61 Port mainwheel
62 Wing fence
63 Wheel housing
64 Retraction jack

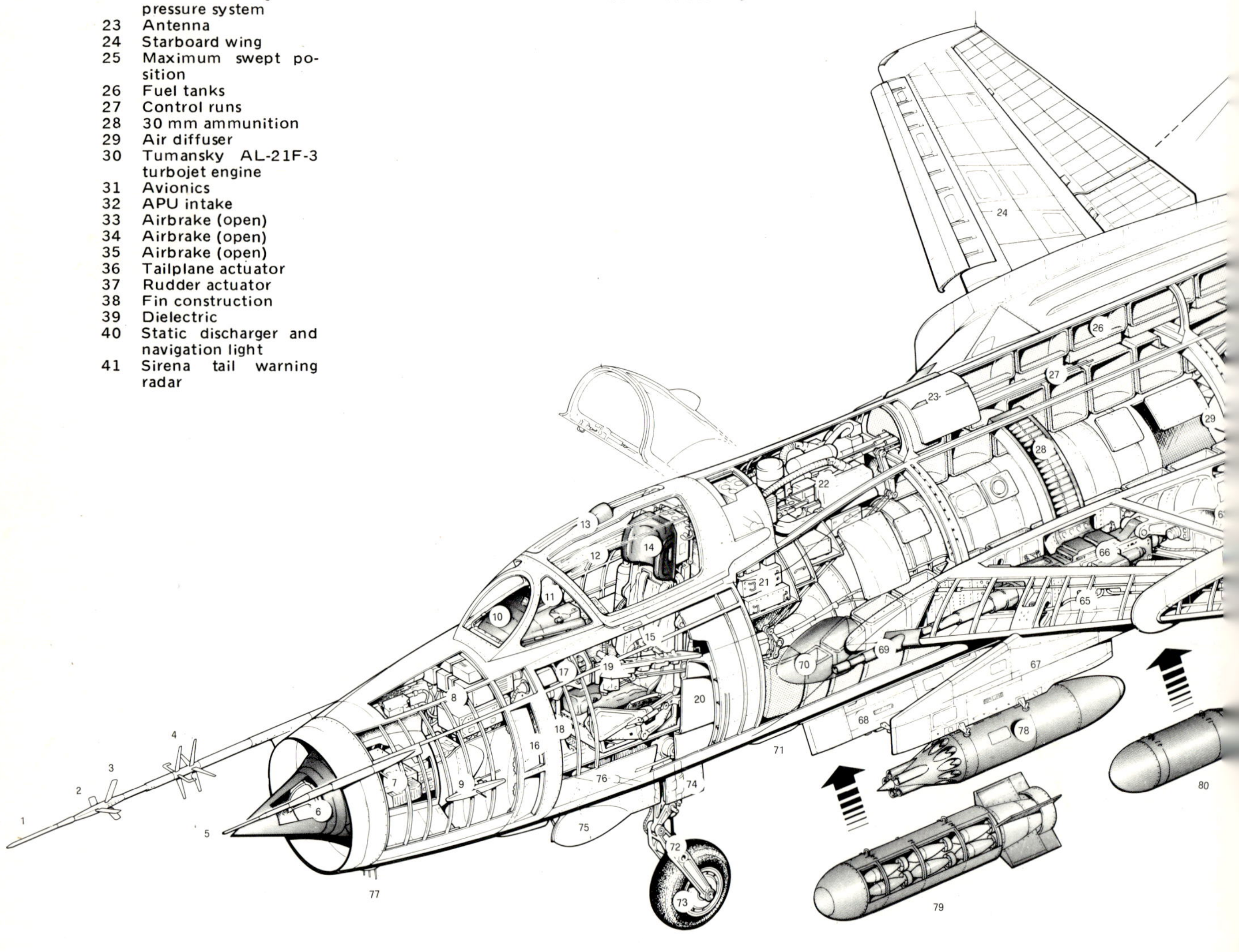

42

Detail drawing key

65 Leading edge construc-
tion
66 Nudelmann-Richter
NR-30 30 mm cannon
67 Pylon
68 Pylon
69 Cannon barrel
70 Cannon blast plate
71 Antenna
72 Nosewheel fork
73 Nosewheel
74 Nosewheel door
75 Nosewheel door
76 Nosewheel housing
77 IFF antennas
78 VU-57B 55 mm ro
ket launcher
79 Cluster bomb
80 GP 250 kg bomb
81 Auxiliary drop tank

82 Antenna
83 Antenna
84 Landing light
85 Glove
86 APU exhausts
87 Inspection hatches
88 Bracke parachute wire
89 Nozzle
90 Tail bumper
91 IFF antennas
92 Antenna
93 Inspection hat-
ches
94 Flap (lowered)
95 Gun camera
96 Radioaltimetre anten-
na
97 Rear fuselage pylons
pair
98 30 mm cannon
99 Front fuselage pylons
pair
100 Doppler radar
101 Landing light
102 Radioaltimetre
103 IFF antennas

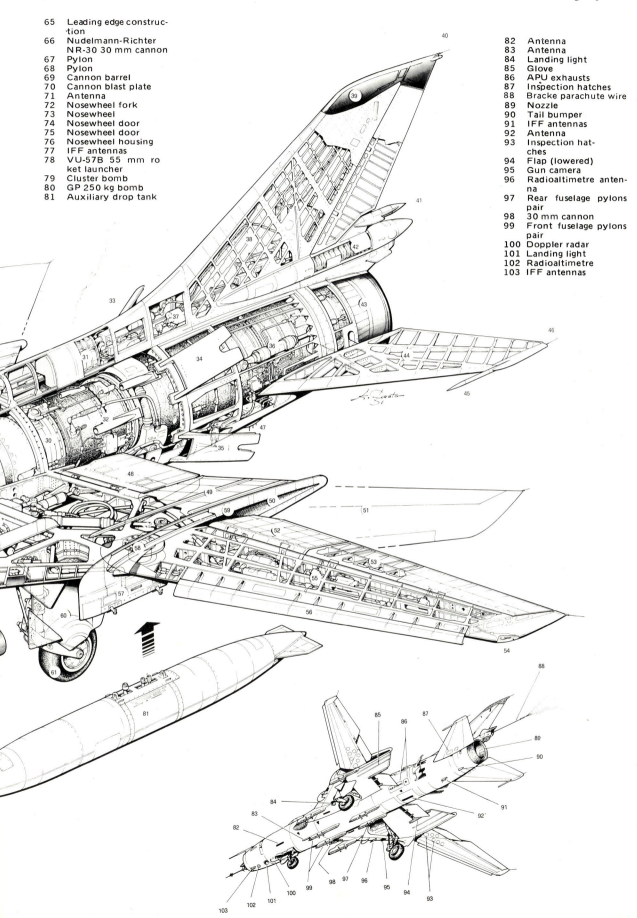

perforating 220 mm (8.66ins) of armour are installed. Su-17s equipped with an external ECM «pod» have been seen and it is probable that they can also carry containers for multi-sensor reconnaissance. This aircraft can also carry the surface-to-air AS-7 Kerry missile besides more sophisticated «smart» type missiles still being developed.

At present approximately 100 Su-17s are in service with the FA (but deliveries are still being made), subdivided into regiments of 35 to 40 aircraft each. 30 Su-20s fit out four squadrons of the Polish Air Force, 36 have been ordered by Peru and at least 8 to 12 examples of the Su-20s are used by Egypt and took part to strike missions against Lybia in July 1977.

Sukhoi Su-17/20 (Fitter-C)
All-weather fighter-bomber, single seat

Power plant: One 76,54 kN (7.800 kg/st, 17,195 lb/st) dry and 109,91 kN (11.200 kg/s, 24,690 lb/st) reheat Lyulka AL-21F-3 axial turbojets. Fuel capacity: 3.700 kg (8,160 lb) or about 4.635 l (1,020 gal).
Dimensions: Wing span 14,00 m (45.93 ft, at 28°), 10,06 m (33 ft, at 62°); length 18,75 m (61.51 ft), without nose probe 17.20 m (56.43 ft); height 4,75 m (15.58 ft); wing area 37,2-40,1 sq m (400-431.6 sq ft).

Weights: Empty 10.000 kg (22,050 lb); loaded 14.000 kg (30,865 lb); maximum take-off (Su-17) 19.000 kg (41,900 lb).

Performance: Maximum speed 2.300 km/h (1,429 mph) at 12.000 m (39,300 ft) (Mach 2.166), 1.300 km/h (808 mph) at sea level (Mach 1.06); initial climb rate 230 m/sec (45,275 ft/min); climb to 11.000 m (36,089 ft) in 1 min 30 sec; service ceiling 18.000 m (59,000 ft); combat radius (lo-lo-lo with 4.000 kg/8,800 lb warload) 200 km (124 mls), (with 2.000 kg/4,400 lb) 360 km (223 mls), (at medium altitude with the same warload) 630 km (391 mls); range (with four external tanks and 1.000 kg/2,200 lb load) 2.170 km (1,348 mls).
Armament: Two forward-firing Nudelmann-Richter NR-30 30-mm cannons in wing roots with 73 rounds per gun and 4.000 kg (8,800 lb) or 5.000 kg (11,000 lb) of external ordnance, respectively for the Su-20 and Su-17.

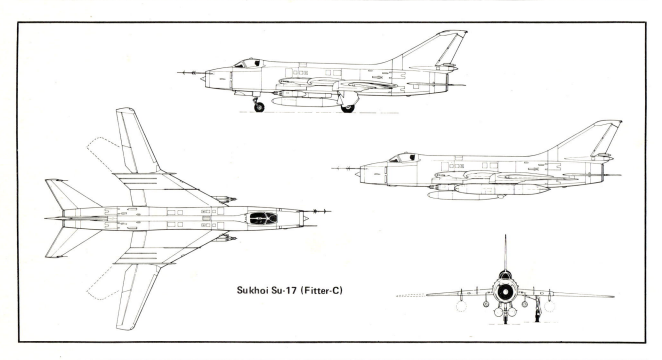

Sukhoi Su-17 (Fitter-C)

Tactical VG aircraft comparison

	Su-20 Fitter-C	MiG-23B Flogger-B	Su-19 Fencer-A	MRCA Tornado	F-111F	F-14A Tomcat
Trust, kg/st	11,200	9,300	26,000	12,240	22,770	18,960
Max wing span, m	14.00	14.25	17.00	13.90	19.20	19.54
Length, m	18.75	16.80	21.50	17.23	22.37	18.89
Height, m	4.75	3.65	—	5.74	5.22	4.87
Max. TO weight	18,000	15,700	30,000	23,000	45,000	31,100
Max. speed Mach	2.17	2.3	2.4	2.1	2.5	2.34
Tactical radius, km	400	350	500	1,000	1,600	725
Range, km	2,170	2,500	—	3,750	6,100	—
Armament, mm	2x30	1x23	2x23	2x27	(1x20)	1x20
Max. bombload, kg	4,000	2,000	4,000	5,000 +	19,400	6,580
Crew	1	1	2	2	2	2

Mikoyan MiG-23 (Flogger)

The Mikoyan E-231, prototype of the MiG-23, was similar to the airframe of the E-230 to which a variable geometry wing was applied. The final project was finished in 1963 and in 1964 the V-VS gave it its approval. In this period both the United States and Eastern Europe were working on variable geometry combat aircraft. The first prototype of the E-231 should have flown in 1966 or 1967, however it was certainly presented to the public in the Domodedovo Air Parade of July 9, 1967, test piloted by Alexander Fedotov. The construction of the aircraft did not present any particular problems and the wing pivot points were selected so that displacement of the wing's aerodynamic centre was avoided during variation of the swept. Once the prototype had undergone several essential modifications, to better the stability, mass production of the aircraft began in 1970 and it was designated MiG-23 (for a time this new aircraft was mistakenly known as the MiG-25 in the West).

The new fighter was powered by a turbojet, however the model and trust are still unknown, which could be a by-product of a Tumansky R-13 or of the Lyulkas. The air intakes are the so-called «Phantom» type with boundary layer control besides two auxiliary intakes per side; the nozzle is a variable geometry converging-diverging type. The fuel system can hold up to 5,000 litres (1,100 gals) of fuel transported internally plus the possibility of installing an auxiliary 600 litre (132 gals) ventral tank which is dropped before using the cannons, and 530 litre (116 gals) transfer tanks which hang from hardpoints on the moveable portion of the wing and prevent variation of the swepts. The fuselage is identical to the one on the E-230 (Faithless) adequately reduced thanks to the removal of the two lift engines and with

space for the principal landing gear. The large radome in the nose contains a fire control radar with an antenna of approximately 85 cm (33.5in) in diameter. There is a Doppler High Lark radar

Some views of the Mikoyan E-231 swing wing fighter, prototype for the MiG-23.

Mikoyan MiG-23S (Flogger-B) cutaway drawing key

1 Pitch sensors and ILS antenna
2 Sirena tail warning radar
3 Static discharger
4 Static discharger
5 Rudder
6 Rudder construction (honeycomb)
7 Fin
8 Dielectric
9 Fin construction and rudder actuators
10 Brake-chute
11 Variable geometry nozzle
12 Nozzle actuators
13 Tailplane pivot
14 Tailplane construction
15 Tailplane (all-moving)
16 Static discharger
17 Maximum wing swept position

18 Air brake (closed)
19 Ventral fin
20 Position of ventral fin folded
21 Airbrake construction
22 Afterburner
23 Fuel tank
24 Fuselage frame
25 Dielectric
26 Assisted take-off rocket
27 Inboard flap
28 Centre flap
29 Honeycomb construction
30 Outboard flap
31 Wingtip construction

32 Navigation light (blue-green)
33 Slat
34 Multispar wing construction
35 AA-7 Apex air-to-air missile
36 K-13A (Atoll) air-to-air missile
37 Underwing ferry tank (with minimum swept only)
38 Starboard mainwheel
39 Mudguard/door
40 L/g leg
41 Mudguard
42 Leading edge horn

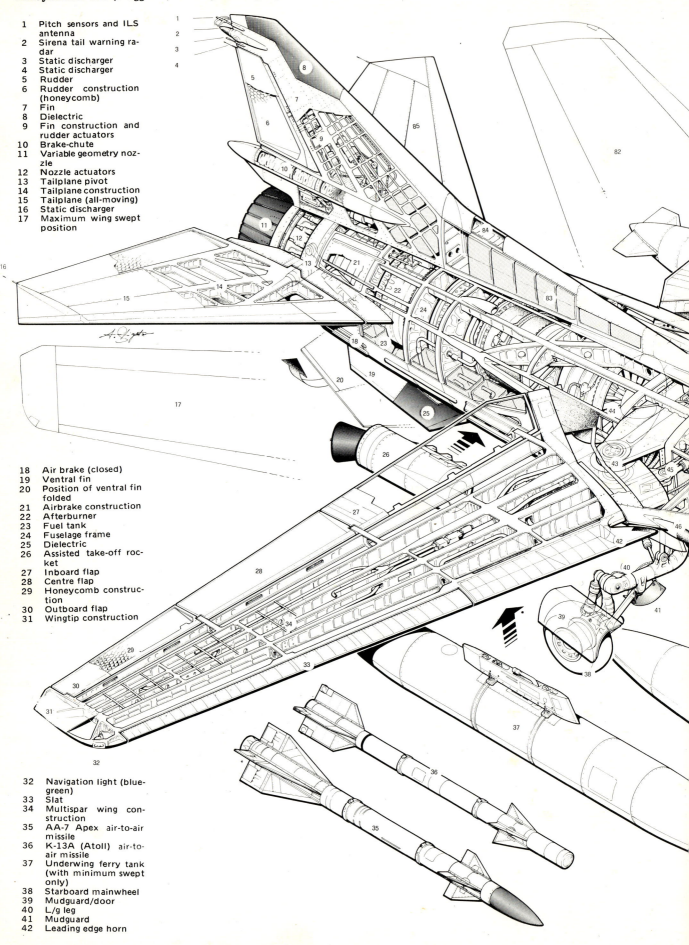

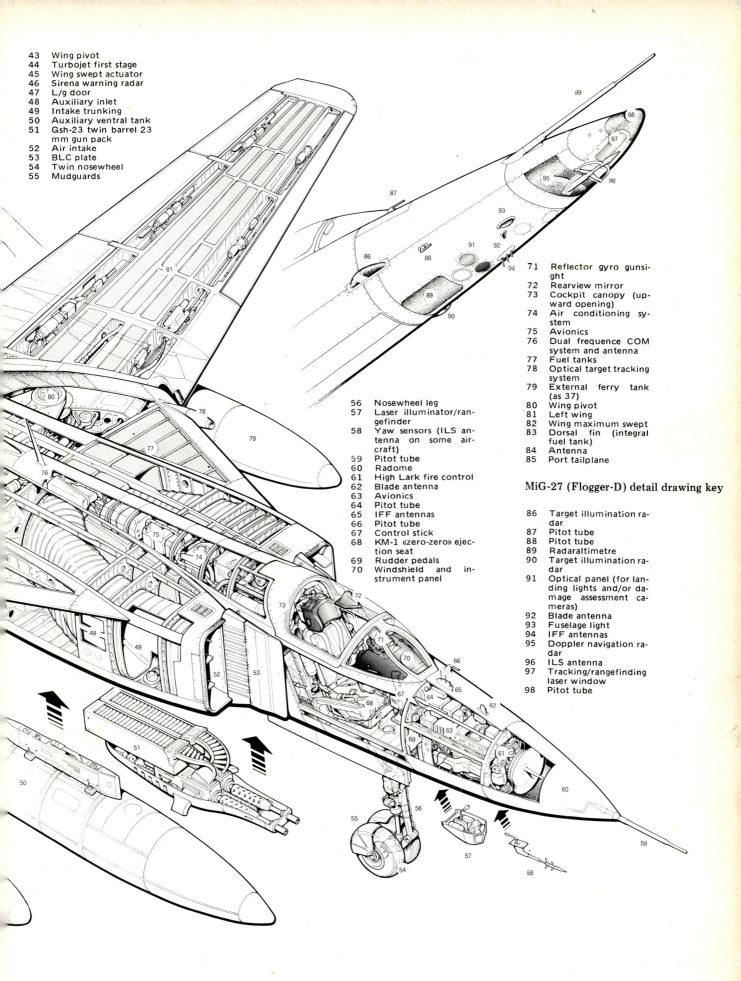

43 Wing pivot
44 Turbojet first stage
45 Wing swept actuator
46 Sirena warning radar
47 L/g door
48 Auxiliary inlet
49 Intake trunking
50 Auxiliary ventral tank
51 Gsh-23 twin barrel 23 mm gun pack
52 Air intake
53 BLC plate
54 Twin nosewheel
55 Mudguards

56 Nosewheel leg
57 Laser illuminator/rangefinder
58 Yaw sensors (ILS antenna on some aircraft)
59 Pitot tube
60 Radome
61 High Lark fire control
62 Blade antenna
63 Avionics
64 Pitot tube
65 IFF antennas
66 Pitot tube
67 Control stick
68 KM-1 «zero-zero» ejection seat
69 Rudder pedals
70 Windshield and instrument panel

71 Reflector gyro gunsight
72 Rearview mirror
73 Cockpit canopy (upward opening)
74 Air conditioning system
75 Avionics
76 Dual frequence COM system and antenna
77 Fuel tanks
78 Optical target tracking system
79 External ferry tank (as 37)
80 Wing pivot
81 Left wing
82 Wing maximum swept
83 Dorsal fin (integral fuel tank)
84 Antenna
85 Port tailplane

MiG-27 (Flogger-D) detail drawing key

86 Target illumination radar
87 Pitot tube
88 Pitot tube
89 Radaraltimetre
90 Target illumination radar
91 Optical panel (for landing lights and/or damage assessment cameras)
92 Blade antenna
93 Fuselage light
94 IFF antennas
95 Doppler navigation radar
96 ILS antenna
97 Tracking/rangefinding laser window
98 Pitot tube

E-231 (prototype), Moscow-Domodedovo, July 1967

MiG-23S (Flogger-B) Soviet V-VS, Eastern Germany, 1974

MiG-23U (Flogger-C) Soviet V-VS, Eastern Germany, 1974

MiG-27 (Flogger-D) Soviet V-VS, Eastern Germany, 1975

MiG-23MS (Flogger-E) LARAF (Lybia), 1976

A pair of MiG-23Ss (Flogger-B) air superiority fighters fitted with laser rangefinder, launching shoes for air-to-air missiles and pylons for free-fall ordnance.

positioned immediately behind, and a laser range-finder, in a protruding fairing, can be installed. The basic MiG-23S version is armed with two Gsh-23 23mm cannons with 100 rounds per gun

Below left, upper: a standard MiG-23S (Flogger-B); lower: another MiG-23S in «all down» configuration. Right: the export version of the MiG-23, allegedly known as MiG-23MS (Flogger-E); the aircraft belongs to the Lybian Air Force.

placed in a fairing behind the wheel wells and it has four hardpoints for air-to-air medium range missiles. The two rails under the external side of the wing carry two AA-7 Apex missiles with alternative radar and infra-red homing, with a range of approximately 22 km (13 mls), while the two hardpoints in the belly of the fuselage are used for two AA-8 Aphyd missiles with infrared rays homing which are suitable for dogfight up to 6.5 - 7.5 km (4 - 4.5 mls). In the MiG-23B, it is possible to apply air-to-air surface light missiles,

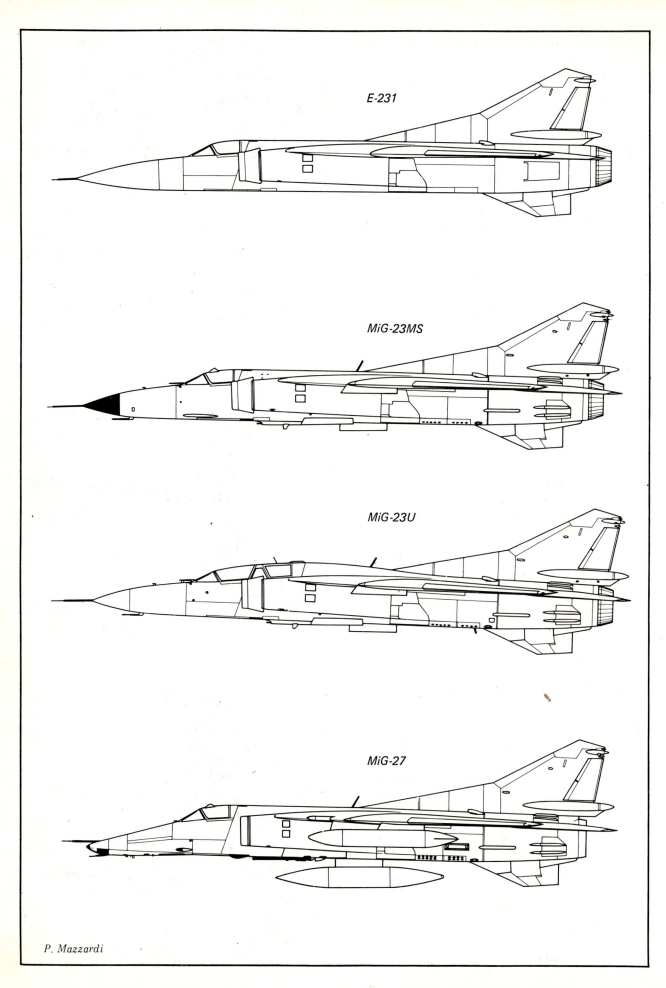

E-231

MiG-23MS

MiG-23U

MiG-27

P. Mazzardi

AS-7 Kerry missiles and «smart bombs» to the last two hardpoints.

At present the MiG-23 is well known in the following versions: MiG-23S (Flogger-B): described in the text, interception version which has a secondary role for ground attack.

MiG-23U (Flogger-C): operational training version, almost identical to the above, which maintains all the combat features even if it has a second seat in tandem (pilot and instructor).

MiG-23R: tactical reconnaissance version. No other information is available.

MiG-27 (Flogger-D) ex-MiG-23B: day ground attack version with a secondary role as air-to-air Fighter. The front part of this aircraft, with a shortened nose, has been completely redesigned in as much as it lacks a fire control and has a Doppler radar, height-finding radar and a laser target tracking system. The air intakes have been simplified as well as the exhaust nozzles, which leaves one to think that the engine installed is similar to the engines in the other versions, but with a less effective afterburner. The armament is made up of a new 23mm cannon with six rotating barrels semiexternally installed and it has a firing rate of 3,000-4,000 shots/min., and four hardpoints — the two central ones have been shifted under the air intakes. The combat load is estimated at approximately 2,000 kg.

MiG-23MS (Flogger-E): this is the export model of the air superiority Flogger-B. The Doppler radar is not adopted and the fire control is equipped with a shorter range radar.

MiG-27 (Flogger-F): export versions of the Flogger-B.

After several Soviet air regiments had adopted the MiG-23s, pre-series version, and evaluated their operational value the first produced examples of Flogger-Bs were assigned to several units of the 16th Tactical Air Force of the Guard in East Germany at the end of 1972. These units, which had previously been fitted with MiG-21MFs, were

Above: a front view of the MiG-27 (Flogger-D) clear-weather fighter-bomber version. Below, upper: the MiG-23U (Flogger-C) conversion trainer; lower: a V-VS MiG-27 landing at an airfield near Berlin, in Eastern Germany.

51

assigned several training MiG-23Us. In 1973 the countries which receive military support from the USSR were ready to receive the new fighter and it seems that the first MiG-23s were spotted above Syrian airports during the last days of the October War and almost contemporarily Egypt also received several examples followed by Iraq and Lybia. Various models of this aircraft were frequently seen in 1974.

Up to and including 1976 the total number of MiG-23s built is estimated between 500 and 1,400 examples; the figure of 1,000 is considered the most probable. Nine or ten examples of this aircraft should be produced each month, and

besides those already in service with the V-VS on Soviet territory (approximately 370) there are 130 through out East Germany. Forty-five MiG-23Bs have been furnished to Syria, approximately 24 MiG-23Ss (or Fs) and as many MiG-23Bs, in addition to several MiG-23Us have gone to Egypt, from 12 to 27 MiG-23Fs and two MiG-23Us to Lybia, 30 MiG-23Bs to Irak and 12 (unconfirmed) to Somalia. This aircraft has also been offered to Finland, which intends to purchase it to substitute its MiG-21Fs, to Peru, which instead bought the Su-22s, and to India, which initially has preferred the MiG-21bis. The cost of the export version aircraft is only 4-5 million dollars.

Mikoyan E-231 MiG-23S (Flogger-B)
All-weather air superiority fighter, with limited ground attack capability, single seat

Power plant: (extimated) one 73,35 kN (7.475 kg/st, 16,480 lb/st) dry and 98.13 kN (10.000 kg/s, 22,045 kg/s) reheat axial turbojet of unspecified type (probably a developed version of the Tumansky R-25 or of the Lyulka AL-21). Fuel capacity: 4.800 l (1,055 gal) and an auxiliary 600 liters (132 gal) belly tank and two 530 l (116 gal) wing tanks (only with 17° swept).

Dimensions: Wing span (17°) 14,00 m (45.93 ft), (71°) 8,50 m (27.88 ft); length 16.15 m (52.98 ft); height 3,95 m (12.96 ft); gross wing area 37,75 sq m (406.33 sq. ft); undercarriage track 4,10 m (13.45 ft).

Weights: Empty about 10.500 kg (23,150 lb); loaded 15.300 kg (33,730 lb); maximum take-off 17.200 kg (37,920 lb).

Performance: Maximum speed 2.336 km/h (1,451 mph) at 11.000 m (36,089 ft) (Mach 2,2), 1.805-1.911 km/h (1,121-1,187 mph) at 11.000 m (36,089 ft) (Mach 1.7-1.8) with 4 AAM, 1.347 km/h

(837 mph) at sea level (Mach 1.1); service ceiling 15.250 m (50,000 ft); combat radius 1.000 km (620 mls); maximum range 2.400 km (1,490 mls), with ferry tanks 2.875 km (1,786 mls).
Armament: A Gsh-23 twin-barrel 23-mm cannon with 100 rounds per barrel, two AA-7 Apex and two AA-9 Aphyd air-to-air missiles.

Mikoyan MiG-27 (Flogger-D)
Day fighter-bomber, single seat

Power plant: as MiG-23S but 93,22 kN (9.500 kg/st, 20,950 lb/st) reheat.
Dimensions: as MiG-23S excepts: length 15,95 m (52.33 ft); height 4,00 m (13.12 ft).
Weights: Empty 10.000 kg (22,000 lb); loaded 16.000 kg (35.275 lb); maximum take-off 17.200 kg (37,900 lb).
Performance: Maximum speed 1.700-1.805 km/h (1,056-1,121 mph) at 11.000 m (36,089 ft) (Mach 1,6-1,7); cruise 850 km/h (528 mph) at 11.000 m (36,089 ft) (Mach 0,8).
Armament: One six-barrel 23-mm cannon of unspecified type and 2.000 kg (4,400 lb) of external loads.

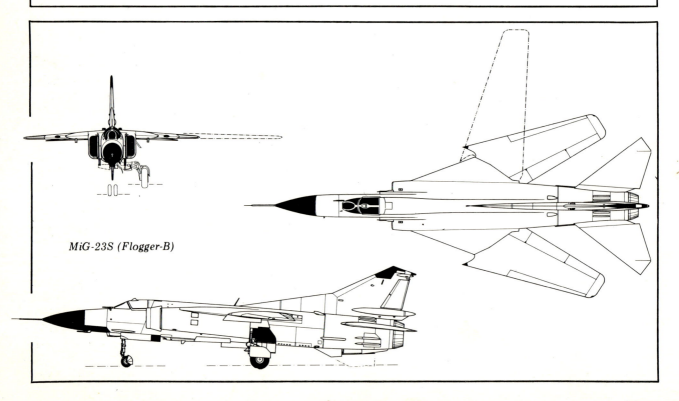

MiG-23S (Flogger-B)

Mikoyan MiG-25 (Foxbat)

The first information which the West obtained of the MiG-25 (Foxbat) did not permit positive identification of the aircraft; in fact, until September 1967, with the escape of Soviet pilot Belenko and his MiG-25P, in no way the West had ever been able to view this aircraft «de visu».

In April 1965 official Soviet sources reported that an E-266 aircraft (the name of the MiG-25 project), powered by two 11,000 kg/s (24,250 lb) «RD» turbojets, piloted by Alexander Fedotov, had established a speed record on a closed circuit of 1,000 km (621 mls) with a payload of 2,000 kg (4,400 lbs) flying the extraordinary average of 2,320 km/h (1,441 mph) at varying altitudes from 21,000 to 22,000 m (68,900 - 72,175 ft). It was thought that the record had been set by an I-152 (then known as a MiG-23 Flipper) or by a special configuration.

Subsequently, four models of a big two-engined jet with twin rudder and bidimensional air intakes were presented at the well known Domodedovo Air Show in the summer of 1967.

These two-engined jets, presented by the official speaker as «Mach 3 interceptor-fighters», were at first mistakenly attributed to Yakovlev and then to Tupolev and still later were erroneously identified as MiG-23s. Instead the aircraft in question were Mikoyan E-266s, pre-series versions of the MiG-25P (Foxbat-A). The misunderstanding — apart from the confusion between MiG-23 and -25 — was however straightened out when, on October 5, 1967, the E-266 and Fedotov returned to the scene setting another sensational record reaching 30,000 m (98,425 ft) after a rocket assisted take-off with payloads of 1,000 and 2,000 kg (2,200 and 4,400 lbs). News agency photographs clearly showed that the twin fin two-engined jet was the one that appeared at Domodedovo.

The requirement which gave origin to the MiG-25 is not well known; however it could be compared to the reasons which brought to the design of the American Lockheed Blackbirds: the need for a long range interceptor which could shoot down American Mach 3 B-70 bombers and noninterceptable spy aircraft.

It seems that, because of the difficulties presented by this request and the apparent presence of only one competitor the project was directly assigned to the Mikoyan staff, with perhaps the assistance of other engineering staffs. The project should have begun somewhere between 1958 and 1961 and the prototypes flew in 1964, or possibly early 1965, and it is believed that they underwent an intensive flight program directed towards studying the entire development of their performance.

The development of the aircraft was, without a doubt, very difficult, so much so that the first pieces of information which regarded the operational service did not reach the West until the early 1970s and they referred to the reconnaissance strategic MiG-25R (Foxbat-B). The first news regarding an operative interception version, the MiG-25P (Foxbat-A), arrived at the end of 1972 from the military information service.

At approximately the same time a two-seat training version was developed — the MiG-25U (Foxbat-C) — which, according to several sources, should have a reduced wing span and according to others, the span should have an increased span; initially, the NATO had identified the Foxbat-C as a ground attack version, and we cannot exclude the possibility that a prototype for this specific purpose was really built, even if the general features of the aircraft do not seem to fit this role.

The MiG-25 was built with a generous amount of stainless steel (even if aluminium and titanium are more widely used than the Eastern press leads us to believe, for example: the leading edges of the wings, the stabilizers, in addition to a large tail section and the exhaust nozzles are made of titanium).

The secret behind its high velocity lies in the two Tumansky R-266 axial flow turbojets (sometimes mistakenly identified or incomplete in form, as RD, R-11, TRD R-31 and TRD R-37F, thereby creating confusion with other Lyulka or Tumansky turbojets which were given the same initials), with a low compression rate and with a single-shaft four stage compressor. Therefore, these engines are not very complicated and have an afterburner and a water and methanol injection cooling system. The avionics, which have miniaturized vacuum tubes rather than semiconductors and printed circuits, are somewhat outdated. The cockpit is pressurized, conditioned and equipped with a KM-1 ejection seat.

The MiG-25P (Foxbat-A Mk.2) model follows the original design of the prototype and it has a Fire Fox fire control with very good power and resistance to the ECMs. All the armaments are exclusively made up of four AA-6 Acrid (ex-Advanced Anab) air-to-air radar type missiles (the two externally carried ones can be infrared versions) with a maximum range of 29 km, however a 23mm gun pod can be installed in the belly.

The MiG-25R (Foxbat-B) varies somewhat from the above version in the shape of its nose, where a high power Jay Bird navigation radar in S Band is mounted along with optical reconnaissance systems (five cameras: three oblique and two vertical), and a side-looking radar (SLAR), etc. Several sources suggest that the MiG-25R varies

Mikoyan MiG-25R (Foxbat-B) cutaway drawing key

1 Nose probe
2 Attitude sensors
3 Radome
4 Radar antenna
5 Jay Bird navigation radar (J-Band)
6 SLAR dielectric
7 Radaraltimetre
8 Doppler radar dielectric
9 Avionics cooling intake
10 Doppler radar
11 Vertical camera
12 Avionics
13 Oblique camera
14 Vertical camera lens
15 Vertical camera
16 Pitot tube
17 Vertical camera lens
18 Vertical camera
19 Instrument panel
20 Windshield

41 Engine combustor
42 Tailplane actuator
43 Tailplane construction
44 Dielectric
45 Rudder hinge
46 Rudder (honeycomb construction)
47 All-moving tailplane
48 Exhaust nozzle
49 Brake-chute housing
50 Fin
51 Rudder
52 Dielectric
53 Sirena 3 tail warning radar
54 Exhaust nozzle
55 Tailplane
56 Ventral fin
57 Dielectric
58 Ventral fin construction

21 KM-1 «zero-zero» ejection seat
22 Seat rocket battery
23 Seat gun
24 Cockpit canopy
25 HF antenna
26 Air intake
27 Navigation light (red)
28 Mobile ramp (electric actuated)
29 Intake trunking
30 Wing strake
31 Wing leading edge construction
32 Multi-spar wing construction
33 Navigation light (red, some batch only)
34 Aileron actuator
35 Aileron construction (honeycomb)
36 Flap actuator
37 Flap (lowered)
38 Fuel (T-6) tank
39 Engine front stage
40 R-266 turbojet compressor

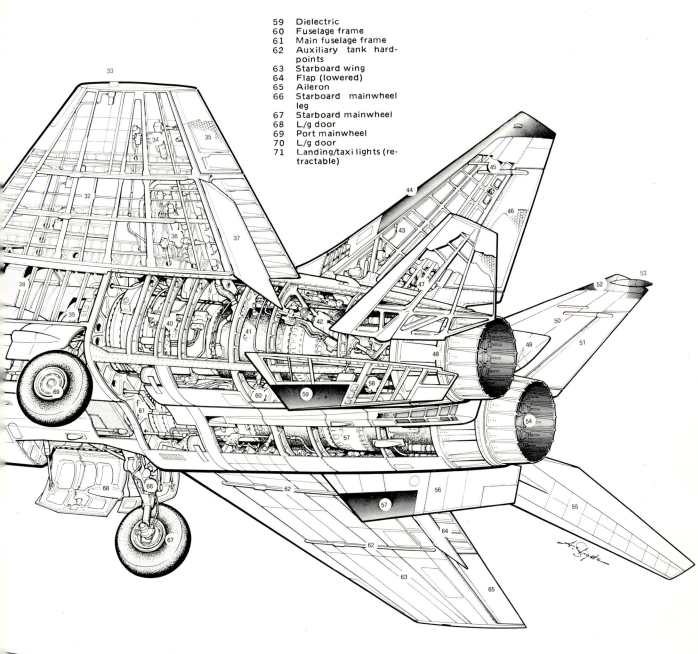

59 Dielectric
60 Fuselage frame
61 Main fuselage frame
62 Auxiliary tank hard-
points
63 Starboard wing
64 Flap (lowered)
65 Aileron
66 Starboard mainwheel
leg
67 Starboard mainwheel
68 L/g door
69 Port mainwheel
70 L/g door
71 Landing/taxi lights (retractable)

MiG-25P (Foxbat-A) drawing key

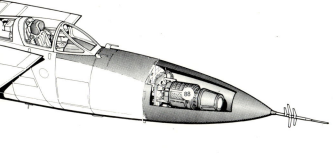

72 Air intake ramp actua-
tor
73 Lower air intake ramp
(take-off position)
74 Twin nosewheel
75 Mudguard
76 Nosewheel leg
77 Nosewheel doors
78 Nosewheel door

79 Brake-chute
80 ECM fairings (optio-
nal)
81 Fuel tanks
82 AA-6 Acrid (IR) mis-
sile (outboard pylons
only)
83 AA-6 Acrid (radar ho-
ming) missile
84 Missile launching shoe
85 Twin-barrel Gsh-23 23
mm cannon (optional)
86 RSIU (Markham) data
link and COM system
87 Air-conditioning sy-
stem
88 Fire Fox fire control

Above: the record-breaker Mikoyan E-266 (Foxbat-A), prototype of the MiG-25 high performance interceptor. Below: a pair of MiG-25P (Foxbat-B) armed with air-to-air Acrid missiles.

from the MiG-25P in that it has a constant swept leading edge and the absence or presence of two ECM fairings at the wing tips. Actually either the

Below: MiG-25P with four missile pylons but without weapons.

information is wrong or else all the MiG-25s now in service adopt the same wing and can do without the ECM fairings.

NATO sources suggest the existence of two other MiG-25 versions: a Foxbat-D with special avionics (which could possibly be used as «pathfinder» and for electronic warfare) and the MiG-25MP (Foxbat-E) a twoseat interceptor version with by two R-266F engines increased in thrust, a fuel system which allows for transportation of up to four great capacity auxiliary tanks (in place of the missiles) thereby permitting an autonomy of five hours and 30 minutes. The MiG-25MP can automatically carry out the entire mission from take-

off to interception and it is equipped with fire control capable of handle 20 targets, identifying 16 and tracking four, even in ground clutter. The armament should allow for the use of other types of missiles and one or two cannons are installed as standard equipment.

All this information was furnished by lieutenant Belenko, but the existence of an E-266M (which should be the MiG-25MP) was already known because on May 17, 1975 Fedotov and Ostapenko had used an aircraft of this type to break the climb records set by the McDonnell-Douglas F-15A *Streak Eagle*.

At present the V-VS should have approximately

Three pre-series E-266.

400 Foxbats (equally divided between interceptors and reconnaissance aircraft) in service; these are supplied to the PVO-Strany and the FA which employ them for reconnaissance flights with an outgoing altitude of 10,500 m and a return altitude of 22,000-25,000 m over Western Europe and the Middle East.

The MiG-25 is unsuitable for evasive or combat manoeuvres (the turn radius and supersonic speed is approximately 40 km), however it is virtually uninterceptable in flight if not without the aid of several types of surface-to-air missiles and special «matched» interceptor-plus-missile (like the F-14A with Phoenix missiles, the F-104S with

The E-266 shows its wing platform and four hardpoints.

AIM-7E or Aspide missiles, the F-15A with AIM-7F missiles) as long as certain favourable conditions are present.

The first regiments (approximately 40 aircraft each) to have the production MiG-25s were organized in the important tactical units of the V-VS — the 16th Tactical Air Force of the Guards stationed in East Germany — the most modern and largest numerically equipped among the 16 Soviet Air Forces.

At one time the Egyptian Air Force had requested a delivery of MiG-25Ps, but today it is not clear whether this request involved the MiG-23s actually delivered. In 1976 a request for Foxbat-As was put in by Iraq, however, at the time of publication this request had not yet been fulfilled.

Mikoyan E-266 MiG-25P (Foxbat-A)
All-weather interceptor fighter, single seat

Power plant: Two 91.26 kN (9.300 kg/st, 20,500 lb/st) dry and 120,70 kN (12.300 kg/st, 27,115 lb/st) reheat with water and methanol injection Tumansky R-266 axial turbojets. Fuel capacity: 17.925 l (3,943 gal).

Dimensions: Wing span 14,17 m (46.49 ft), (without wingtips ECM fairings) 14,00 m (45.93 ft); length 23,82 m (78.15 ft), (without noseprobe) 22.30 m (73.16 ft); height 6.10 m (20.01 ft); wing area 56,83 sq m (611.71 sq ft); undercarriage track 3,97 m (13.02 ft).

Weights: Empty 19.000 kg (41,900 lb); loaded (with 4 AAM) 30.920 kg (68,165 lb); maximum take-off 35.000 kg (77,150 lb).

Performance: Maximum speed 3.398 km/h (2.111 mph) at 19.200 m (63,000 ft) (Mach 3,2); maximum continuous speed 2.973 km/h (1,847 mph) at 16.750 m (55,000 ft) (Mach 2,8), 1.037 km/h (644 mph) at 300 m (1,000 ft) (Mach 0,85); climb to 11.000 m (36,089 ft) in 2 min 30 sec (7 min 50 sec without reheat); service ceiling 22.500-25.000 m (73,000-82,000 ft); absolute ceiling 30.000 m (98,500 ft); combat radius 440-560 km (273-348 mls); normal range 980-1.295 km (609-804 mls).

Armament: a modified GP-9 gun pod with a Gsh-23 twin-barrel 23-mm cannon with about 300 rounds (optional) and four AA-6 Acrid (former AA-6-2 Advanced Anab) air-to-air missiles.

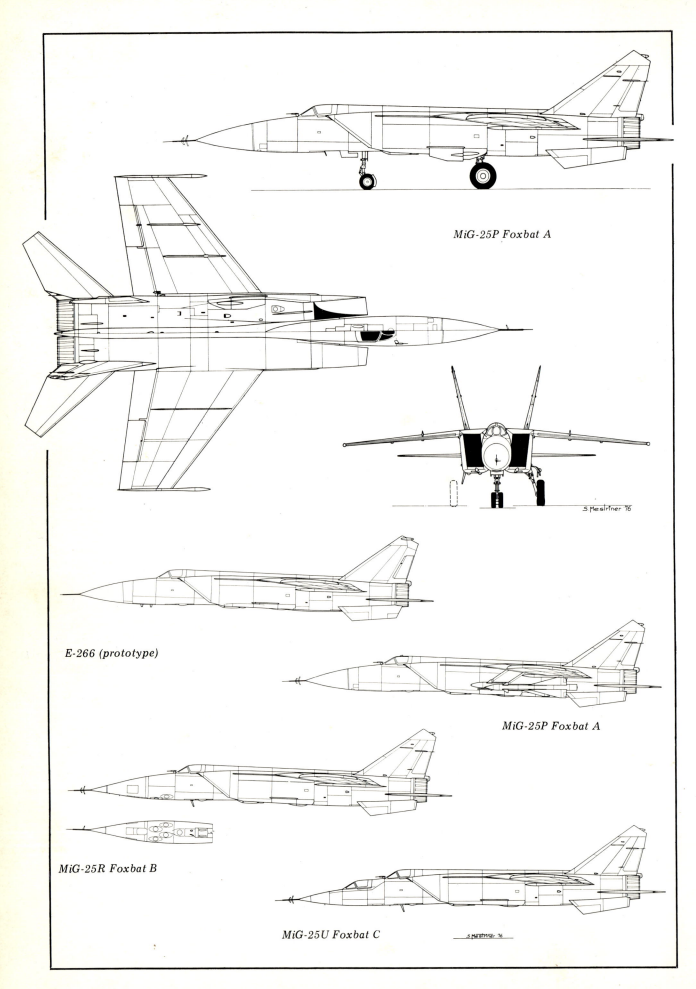

MiG-25P Foxbat A

S. Mestriner '76

E-266 (prototype)

MiG-25P Foxbat A

MiG-25R Foxbat B

MiG-25U Foxbat C

S. Mestriner '76

Sukhoi Su-19 (Fencer)

The most recent Soviet combat aircraft — the Sukoi Su-19 (Fencer-A) — entered service in 1976 but it will not be in full operative capacity until 1978.

The first positive identification of one of the most significant Soviet aircraft for tactical ground attack was had at the beginning of 1974 from the Joint Chief of Staff of the U.S. Armed Forces, Admiral Thomas H. Moorer, who described it as «the first modern Soviet fighter to be developed specifically as fighter-bomber for the ground attack mission». Actually, rumours of «a variable geometry version of the Flagon» had been circulating for over a year, in as much as spy satellites had already photographed the Fencer, but the western press had initially confused it with the Su-17.

Little or nothing is known about the development of this aircraft, but it is believed that a prototype flew in 1972. In NATO circles it is classified as a fighter; however, it is really an aircraft in the U.S. F-111 class.

Its design is taken from the Su-15, maintaining, almost untouched, the same fuselage, except for its front portion and the cockpit, and probably the vertical fin. It has sometimes been represented with a large front radome (as that of the Su-15) or with a short nose, like the MiG-27 one. Therefore, it is possible that a multipurpose (air superiority and ground attack) version was developed and another more specifically suitable for interdiction, as also happened with the MiG-23.

The Su-19 seems to be the aircraft most endowed with the richest series of avionics and with the most modern and flexible armaments which were produced in the USSR, as it can also use AS-8 and AS-X-10 smart bombs, antiradar AS-X-9 missiles or two new types of ASMs weighing approximately 1,250 kg (2,750 lbs). In flight the Fencer will be refuelled by a new air tanker derived from the II-76, presently being developed, and it can employ auxiliary tanks holding up to approximately 1,250 litres (275 gals) of fuel.

In 1974 the first regiment (polk) of the FA, for operative trials, with pre-series Su-19s was formed and it was called the «Tcherniakovski» Polk. At the end of the summer of 1976 a second regiment was formed assigned to the 16th Tactical Air Army and stationed at Lusatia in East Germany.

Sukhoi Su-19 (Fencer-A)
All-weather fighter-bomber, two seater

Power plant: Two 76,54 kN (7.800 kg/st, 17,195 lb/st) dry and 101.91 kN (11.200 kg/st, 24,690 lb/st) Lyulka AL-21F-3 axial turbojets. Fuel capacity (extimated): 9.700 kg (21,385 lb) or about 12.155 l (2,675 gal) and two 1.250 l (275 gal) auxiliary tanks.
Dimensions: Maximum wing span 17,15 m (56.26 ft), minimum 9,53 m (31.26); length 21,29 m (69.85 ft); height 6.20 m (20.34 ft); wing area 40,60-56,30 sq m (437,0-606,0 ft).
Weights: (approx.) Empty 18.300 kg (40,300 lb); loaded 28.000-29.500 kg (61,600-64,900 lb); maximum take-off 30.850-35.500 kg (68,000-78,100 lb).
Performance: Maximum speed 2.608 km/h (1,620 mph) at 11.000 m (36,089 ft) (Mach 2,4), 1.347 km/h (837 mph) at sea level (Mach 1,1); initial climb rate over 250 m/sec (49,000-50,000 ft/min); service ceiling 19.000 m (62,500 ft); combat radius 350-1.950 km (217-1,211 mls); range 4.500 km (2,800 mls).
Armament: 7.500 kg (16,500 lb) of ordnance and (optional) a twin-barrel 23 mm cannon (air superiority) with 100-150 rounds per barrel or a six rotating barrel 23 mm-gun (interdiction).

A so-called «photograph» that possibly depicts a model or is, simply, an artist's impression.

Tupolev Tu-28 (Fiddler)

Even though the Tupolev Tu-28 (Fiddler) is a combat aircraft with many important features, it is one of the least known among the Soviet operative aircraft. This aircraft was first photographed by a U-2 spy aircraft of the CIA in 1959 and due to its obvious resemblance to the Tupolev Tu-98 (Backfin) it was taken for a new medium supersonic bomber developed from the preceeding, and acquired the code name Blinder. During the 1961 Aviation Day matters complicated when the Tu-105 was also presented and this was the authentic medium bomber derived from the Backfin and destined to replace the Tu-16 (Badger), temporarily identified as Beauty. Therefore, an exchange of names took place also because the real roles of the two aircraft were identified: the Tu-102 or Tu-28 became the Fiddler and the Tu-105 or Tu-22 was called Blinder. The Tu-102/Tu-28 originated in 1955 when a request was issued for a replacement of the

The Fiddler is rapidly being phased out of front line V-VS service.

The Tupolev Tu-28P (Fiddler-B), armed with Ash missiles, is the world's largest fighter.

Yak-25 with greater autonomy and having the primary function of an all-weather interceptor. Certainly both the Lavochkin La-250 Anaconda and the Tupolev Tu-102 (Fiddler-A) took part in the competition. It is believed that the La-250 was the first to be completed, flying in the first half of 1956, but after two accidents, which occured in June 1956 and November 1959, the project was abandoned. Instead the Tu-102 flew in late 1956 and presented less problems, being able to pass the preliminary tests in 1959 (this is the given opinion). At least one or two prototypes were built and presented, as said above, at Tushino in 1961.

The aircraft was powered by two Lyulka AL-7 turbojets and it featured a large canoe-shaped ventral radome containing a search «snap-down» radar with low sensitivity to fixed ground-clutter. Therefore, the aircraft should have carried out the «hunter-killer» mission, i.e., both search and destruction of the target. Destruction was accomplished by means of two air-to-air radar guided AA-5 Ash missiles — the first Soviet long range arms of this type.

This solution evidently had to be given up in as much as the V-VS abandoned the autonomous «modus operandi» preferring to entrust its Tu-28s to ground or airborne control. Therefore, in 1967, the production version of this all-weather fighter was presented to the public — the Tu-28P (Fiddler-B) without a large ventral radome (and the two ventral fins), and with double armaments which were improved in flexibility with the introduction of the AA-5 Ashes having an infrared homing.

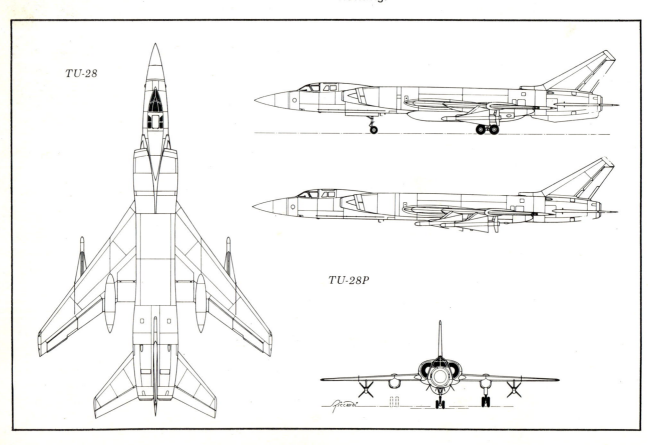

TU-28

TU-28P

Even if the Fiddler has considerably superior proportions (it is, without question, one of the biggest fighter aircraft ever built) it can be paralleled to the American F-102 and as such, therefore, rapidly outdated, so much so that in 1974 it seems to have been flanked and was then progressively replaced by the Tu-128, an interceptor version of the Tu-22 (Blinder).

It is believed that the Tu-28's primary function was to patrol zones which were left partially uncovered by the SAM «umbrella»; this was possible thanks to its capacity to remain in the air for up to three hours 30 minutes without auxiliary tanks and in-flight refuelling. Its fire control depends on a Big Nose radar of considerable range and probably, during production, its power plant developed as did those of the Sukhoi fighters (AL-7F, AL-7F-1 and possibly AL-21F-3).

The total number of aircraft in service is estimated at between 130 and 400.

Tupolev Tu-102 Tu-28P (Fiddler-B)
All-weather long range interceptor fighter, two seat.

Power plant: Two 68,69 kN (7.000 kg/st, 15,400 lb/st) dry and 107,95 kN (11.000 kg/st, 24,250 lb/st) reheat Lyulka AL-7F-1 axial turbojets. Fuel capacity: at least 18.500 l (4,070 gal).
Dimensions: Wing span 19,30 m (63.32 ft); length 27,25 m (89.40 ft); height 5,83 m (19.13 ft).
Weights: (approx.) Loaded 30.000 kg (66,000 lb); maximum take-off 45.000 kg (99,000 lb).
Performance: Maximum speed 1.840 km/h (1,143 mph) at 11.000 m (36,089 ft) (Mach 1.73), with four AAM 1.634 km/h (1,015 mph) (Mach 1.54); cruise 1.015 km/h at 11.000 m (36,089) (Mach 0,95); service ceiling 16.000 m (52,500 ft); combat radius 900-1.440 km (560-895 mls); range 3.450 km (2,145 mls).
Armament: Four AA-5 Ash air-to-air missile (two radar and two IR homing).

Tupolev Tu-126 (Moss)

The Tupolev 126 (Moss) airborne early warning aircraft, known in the US as the SUAWACS and in Pakistan as «the spider».

The Tupolev Tu-126 (Moss), for a time identified by the American Department of Defense as SUAWACS (Soviet Union AWACS) and by the Pakistani intelligence service as The Spider, is the early warning airborne radar version of the Tupolev Tu-114 Rossiya (Cleat). The airframe of the Tu-114 was hardly touched and a saucer shaped rotating radome with a diameter of 11 m (36.09 ft) was installed on the modified fuselage. This change was similar to the solution adopted for the western Lockheed Warning Stars, the AWACS and the Hawkeye.

News of the Tu-126 came out towards the middle of the 1960s, and in 1968 confirmation was had with the release of a colored documentary film which showed this aircraft. It entered service between 1967 and 1970 replacing the traditional fighter ground control. The aircraft, whose functions are parallel to those of the western AEW aircraft, mainly operates in liaison with the Fiddlers, Flagons and Foxbats of the air defence; but obviously it can guide operations for the MiG-21 air superiority and Su-17 ground attack aircraft. According to Pakistani sources a Tu-126 should have lead the operations of the Indian fighters during the last conflict, while other sources do not exclude that aircraft of this type collaborated with the Arab Air Forces during the recent Arab-Israeli War.

At present the V-VS has 10-12 Tu-126s at its disposal, and it seems that two or three examples have also been assigned to the AV-MF.

The characteristics and technical data closely resemble those of the Tu-114s, Tu-114Ds, and Tu-95s except for the maximum cruise speed estimated at 740 km/h (460 mph), a maximum range without in-flight refuelling of approximately 6,500 km (over 4,000mls) and a total weight of 163,000 kg (359,350lbs).

Tupolev Tu-16 (Badger)

Tupolev Tu-16 (Badger-B) maritime reconnaissance aircraft shadowing the British aircraft carrier Ark Royal.

In 1951 Tupolev began working on a new medium jet bomber similar to the American Boeing B-47. It was called the Tu-88 twin jet which was also referred to as Samolet N (N aircraft) during its development period.

The Ilyushin Il-46 was presented in this competition along with the Tu-88; however it had no follow-up. The Central Institute of Aerodynamics contributed to the development of the new fighter with wing swept and it referred to this project as TsAGI-288. Western intelligence services first identified the aircraft as Type 39 and then as Badger; however they ·were later perplexed on the aircraft's paternity, but this doubt was soon removed when the Tupolev Tu-104, the passenger counterpart of the Badger, officially appeared.

The Tu-88 (known in V-VS circles as the Tu-16) was rapidly developed and the prototype had already flown in 1952; mass production began in November 1953. Official presentation of the aircraft followed in the Tushino Air Show of May 1, 1954 in which nine Tu-16s took part, while on

Aviation Day of the following year several formations totalling 54 bombers paraded, demonstrating that the ADD units (Strategic Air Forces) were already equipped with a new powerful medium bomber.

The prototypes and the pre-production aircraft were mounted with two eight-stage 66.24 kN (6,750 kg/s, 14,880 lb/st) Mikulin RD-3 turbojets and then substituted by the 93.23 kN (9,500 kg/s, 20,940 lb/st) AM-3M (or RD-3M) turbojets on the production aircraft.

The armament consisted of two remotely-controlled turrets with a pair of 23mm cannons, a similar type of tail station and another cannon on the right side of the nose, plus 9,000 kg (19,800 lbs) of bombload in the spacious bomb bay.

Because of its capacities as an oceanic reconnaissance-aircraft the Marine Air Force considered it ideal for its cruise missiles. The following versions are known in the West:

Badger-A: this is the first production bombing version described in the text; it was assigned to the Air Forces of China (which undertook a limited

From top to below: two Tu-16 (Badger-As) practicing the wing tip to wing tip inflight refuelling system. The Badger-B was the first version with ASM missiles. The Badger-D with its large nose radome.

production), Egypt (all examples, 20-30, destroyed in the Six Day War), and Iraq (six examples). Several were converted into air tankers and others have been used for training and meteorological reconnaissance.

Badger-B: first missile carrier version armed with two AS-1 Kennel missiles; it served with the AV-MF and the Air Forces of Indonesia, Egypt and Iraq. It differs from the Badger-A because of its two wing hardpoints for missiles and a large retractable guide radar in mid-fuselage.

Badger-C: the name was previously assigned to the maritime reconnaissance model; now it refers to the version armed with an AS-2 Kipper missile half externally carried in the bomb bay. This version was never exported.

Badger-D: Maritime reconnaissance version with a large front radome and three small ventral radomes, one of which is retractable. It is still in service and seems to have flown under Egyptian colours and with Soviet crews. It appeared in 1961.

Badger-E: strategic reconnaissance version of the Badger-A which features a photocamera in the bomb bay.

Badger-F: the Badger-E version featuring two subwing pods with electronic apparatus which, it is thought, are employed for telemetry and in connection with naval missile guidance.

Badger-G: Badger-B version armed with AS-5 Kelt missiles. Eighteen examples were used by the

Egyptian Air Force during the Yom Kippur War and one was shot down.

1,500 to 2,000 examples of the Tupolev Tu-16

The Badger-F is fitted with two underwing pods supposedly connected with targeting of Shaddock class cruise missiles.

were built. Russia has ceased their production, whereas China began building this model in the early 1970s so that it would be its standard atomic carrier until the balistic missiles entered service. The V-VS and AV-MF have progressively replaced this aircraft with the Tu-22 (Blinder). At the present time the USSR still has 450 models in service. In other countries the Tu-16s are distributed as follows: China (60-100), Egypt (17-25), Indonesia (22-nonactive), Iraq (8-9), Libya (at least 12).

Tupolev Tu-16 (Badger-D)
Strategic medium bomber with 7-man crew

Power plant: Two 93,23 kN (9.500 kg/s, 20,940 lb/st) Mikulin AM-3M RD-3M axial turbojets.
Dimensions: Wing span 33,50 m (109.91 ft); length 36,80 m (120.73 ft); height 10,80 m (35.43 ft); wing area 169,0 sq m (1,819.1 sq ft).
Weights: Loaded 68.000 kg (149,900 lb); maximum take-off 77.000 kg (169,750 lb).

Performance: Maximum speed 945 km/h (587 mph) at 10.700 m (35,000 ft) (Mach 0,885); cruise 786 km/h (488 mph) at 12.000 m (39,300 ft); service ceiling 13.000 m (42,700 ft); range 6.400 km (3,975 mls).
Armament: Six Nudelmann-Richter NR-23 23-mm cannons in three turrets and no external or internal warload. Other versions carry 9.000 kg (19,800 lb) of ordnance, two AS-1 Kennel/AS-5 Kelt or one AS-2 Kipper air-to-surface missiles.

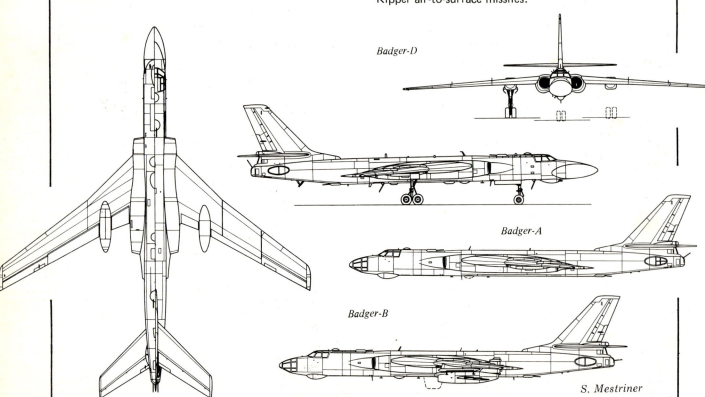

Badger-D

Badger-A

Badger-B

S. Mestriner

64

Myasischev Mya-4 (Bison)

At the moment the only operational version of the Mya-sischev M-4 four-jet bomber is the maritime reconnaissance 201M (Bison-C).

The Mya-4 or M-4 (TsAGI-428 for the Central Institute of Aerodynamics) was born as an alternative to the Tupolev Tu-95 (Tu-20) four turbo-props classed with the American Boeing B-52.
Since its design was similar to that of the Tu-16 (when it was heard of in the West it was immediately attributed to Ilyushin) the Western press tagged this bomber with the initials II-38, whereas the NATO defined it Type 37; the units referred to it as Molot (hammer).
The development phase was approximately parallel to that of the Tu-16 and this aircraft was the last successful project carried out by Vladimir M. Myasischev. The M-4 was first presented at the Tushino Air Show of May 1, 1954 and it probably flew for the first time in the summer of 1953, afterwhich it received a go-shead for production with an accelerated rate of 15 models per month. The results were not 100% satisfactory, above all for the fuel consumption of the 4 Mikulin RD-3M turbojets which limited its range without in-flight refuelling (developed later in the USSR), and therefore the production was contained. The exact number is not available but without a doubt it is under 500 models (some estimates speak of 150-200).

Beginning with late 1959 several M-4s were modified to receive the new Soloviev D-15 turbofans and they were assigned to the Naval Air Force. Official Soviet sources have named this version the 103-M and 201-M. Developed for strategic reconaissance, it has a bomb bay partially occupied by electronic apparatus and partially by space predisposed for the installation of in-flight probe and drogue refuelling equipment. The armament has been reduced from five to three turrets. Contemporaneously, a third version for oceanic reconnaissance was created (presented in 1967 at Domodedovo), which is only distinguishable by the shape of its nose which lodges a Puff Ball Radar in X-band.
This version has never been exported and given the failure of the M-52 (Bounder), a substitute has never been found. At present there are 35 examples in service.

Myasischev M-4 Molot (Bison-A)
Strategic heavy bomber with 7-8 man crew.

Power plant: Four 93,23 kN (9.500 kg/s, 20,940 lb/st) Mikulin AM-3M RD-3M axial turbojets.
Dimensions: 52,0 m (170.5 ft); length 49,50 m (162.40 ft); height 12,20 m (39.96 ft).
Weights: Loaded 160.000 kg (353,000 lb).
Performance: Maximum speed 1.000 km/h (621 mph) at 3.000 m (10,000 ft) (Mach 0,846), 900 km/h (559 mph) at 11.000 m (36,089 ft) (Mach 0,847); service ceiling 12.200-13.700 m (40,000-45,000 ft); range 9.650 km (6,000 mls).
Armament: Eight Nudelmann-Richter NR-23 23 mm-cannons in four turrets and 9.000 kg (19,800) load of nuclear and conventional free-fall bombs.

Myasischev 201-M (Bison-C)
Strategic and maritime reconnaissance/tanker aircraft
Weights: maximum take-off 185.000 kg (408,000 lb).
Performance: Maximum speed 1.012 km/h (629 mph) at 3.000 m (10,000 ft) (Mach 0,857), 955 km/h (594 mph) at 12.000 m (39,300 m) (Mach 0,9); cruise 835 km/h (519 mph) at 12.000 m (39,300 ft) (Mach 0,786); service ceiling 13.000 m (43,000 ft); maximum endurance 15 h.
Armament: Six Nudelmann-Richter NR-23 23-mm cannons in three turrets.

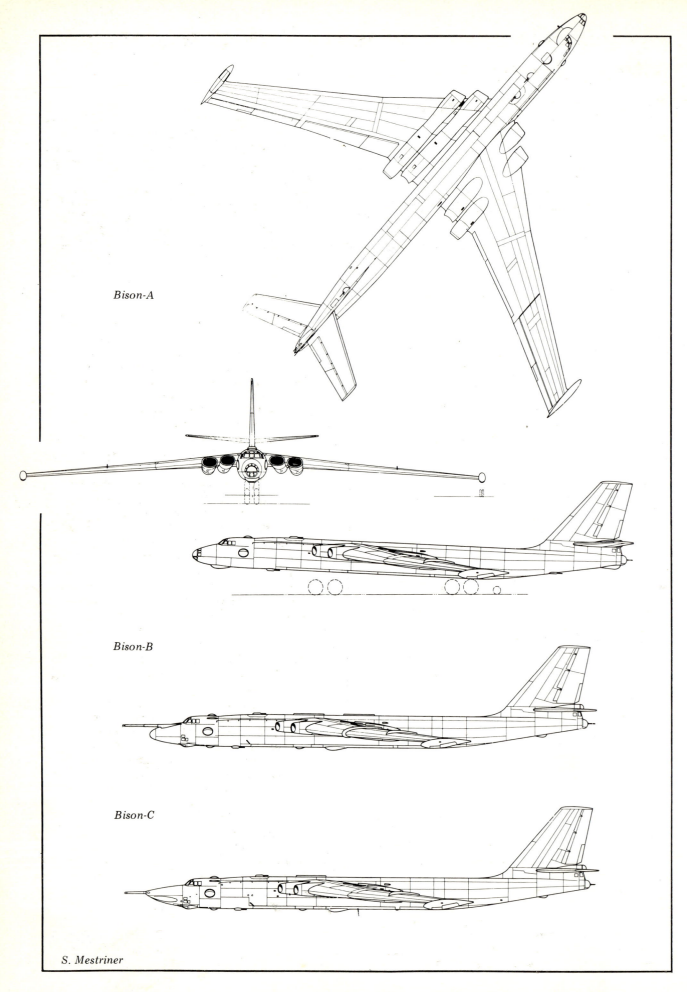

Bison-A

Bison-B

Bison-C

S. Mestriner

Tupolev Tu-20 (Bear)

The Tupolev Tu-20 (Bear-D, project designation Tu-95), one of fastest turboprop-driven aircraft in the world.

In design the Tupolev Tu-95 (in service known as the Tu-20 and Bear for the NATO) is similar to the Myasischev Mya-4 Molot (Bison) and to the Tupolev Tu-16 (Badger) and it clearly shows the hand of the ZAGI in its preparation. This final link, in a series of strategic bombers planned by Tupolev and based on the American Boeing B-29, was designed in 1953 to furnish the Strategic Command of the V-VS with an intercontinental bomber similar to the American B-36 and B-52. Therefore, the range problems which were present in the similar Mya-4 were resolved.

The collectivity of the «builder» Tupolev adapted the Tu-85 (Barge) fuselage, the last piston-engined derivation of the B-29 or Tu-4 (Bull), to a wing swept. In order to overcome the inconveniences created by the tremendous fuel consumption of the big axial turbojets, the Defense Minister turned to Dipl. Engineer Ferdinand Brandner (whose name was also connected with the Egyptian E-300 and Indian Marut) and together with the «builder» Nikolai D. Kuznetsov developed the more than 12,000HP NK-12M.

Powered by four turboprops of this type, featuring counterrotating four blade props which have a rather high rotating speed (a peripherical velocity of 700-875 km/h (435-543 mph) i.e., between Mach 0.66 and Mach 0.82) the Tu-20 can achieve velocity performances close to those of jet bombers of its own generation the ceiling of Mach 1,08 was reached on the test bed.

The Tu-20 (Bear-A) first flew in the late summer of 1954 and was presented at Tushino in July 1955. By the second half of 1956 it had already been put into service with the ADD or DA (Strategic Air Force).

By installing a new larger diameter fuselage on the Tu-20 Tupolev was able to create the Tu-114 Rossiya (Cleat for the NATO), and approximately 30-35 models of this version were used by the Aeroflot up until 1975. The Tu-114D (Dalnii, wide range) which was directly taken from the Bear-A, flew for the first time in August of 1957 and in the spring of 1958 it covered the Moscow-Irkutsk-Moscow 8,500 km (5,280 ml) route avera-

ging 810 km/h (503 mph, approximately Mach 0.76), thereby indirectly confirming the performance of this bomber. A very specialized military version, the Tu-126 (in code first known as AUAWACS or the Soviet Union's AWACS and later as Moss), was derived from the civilian Tu-114 model. This model was destined for radar warning and airborne control.

Other versions with special functions which were developed from the Tu-95/20 (Bear-B) are listed below:

Bear-B: the «flying cruiser» version armed with an AS-3 Kangaroo surface-to-air missile with a range of 650 km (405 mls) lodged in a bay with a modified hatch was introduced in 1961. The Bear-Ds were equipped with a probe for in-flight refuelling and several have a radome on the left side of the fuselage.

Bear-C: destined for strategic reconnaissance and maritime surveillance the Bear-C corrisponds to the preceeding versions (and it is possible that it was obtained for conversion) but the use of a «cruise» missile is impossible as its bay must lodge electronic apparatus. All models have radomes on both sides of the fuselage. The Bear-D was first signaled out in 1964.

Bear-D: this version was first identified in the summer of 1967 by an icebreaker of the USCG. It derives its design from the Bear-A, however it is recognizable by its in-flight refuelling probe, a navigation radar with an enlargened antenna, a large ventral radome with a Puff Ball radar for missile tracking and guidance of class Shaddock naval cruisers, two radomes at the sides of the fuselage and a new rear alarm radar. Numerous antennas and dielectrics betray the enrichened electronic equipment. 15,000 CV NK-12MA engines are installed. The aircraft is immediately identified by two fairings at the tips of the tailplanes.

Bear-E: photographic reconnaissance version of the above, it is practically identical except for the presence of six or seven cameras in the bay in place of the radome for the Puff Ball and the absence of the two fairings at the tips of the tailplanes. It is believed that strengthened motors are installed.

Bear-F: characterized by two enlarged fairings for the nacelles of the internal engine; this ulterior modification, which appeared in 1973, proves that the distribution of the various radomes was not very rigid and it is considered destined for target tracking and guidance of naval «cruise» missiles. The Bear-E does not have the two lateral radomes and a ventral turret. The engines are the same as those of the last version.

The importance of the Tu-20 as a bomber has greatly declined. American figures estimated the presence of 100 Bear-Bs in service in 1975-1976, and these were destined to be substituted by the new Backfire-Bs in 1977. The AV-MF remains the biggest user of the «electronic» versions with approximately 50 -C, -D, -E and -Fs indispensable for enemy fleet surveillance, target tracking and guidance of «cruise» missiles against these. In 1976 the Tu-126s numbered about 12, but it seems that this figure will increase.

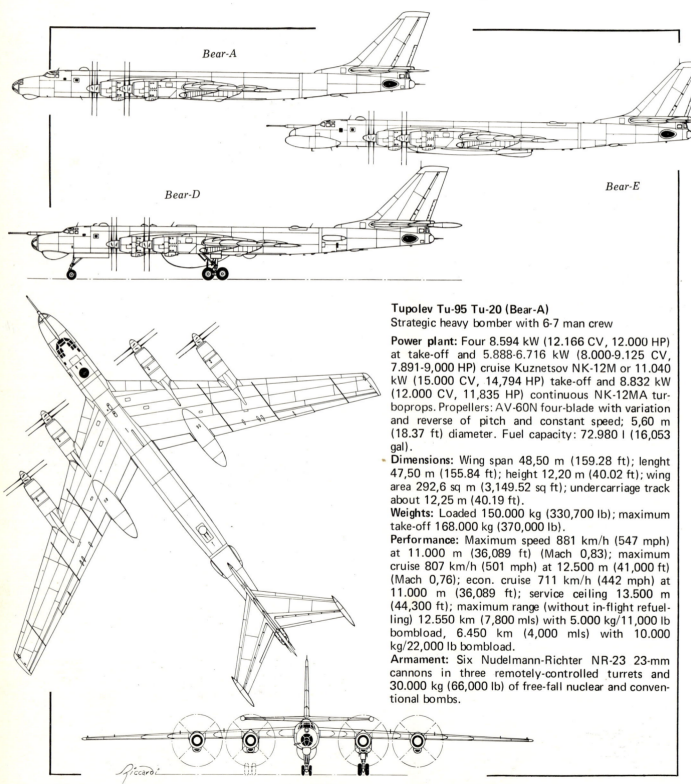

Bear-A

Bear-D

Bear-E

Tupolev Tu-95 Tu-20 (Bear-A)
Strategic heavy bomber with 6-7 man crew

Power plant: Four 8.594 kW (12.166 CV, 12.000 HP) at take-off and 5.888-6.716 kW (8.000-9.125 CV, 7.891-9,000 HP) cruise Kuznetsov NK-12M or 11.040 kW (15.000 CV, 14,794 HP) take-off and 8.832 kW (12.000 CV, 11,835 HP) continuous NK-12MA turboprops. Propellers: AV-60N four-blade with variation and reverse of pitch and constant speed; 5,60 m (18.37 ft) diameter. Fuel capacity: 72.980 l (16,053 gal).

Dimensions: Wing span 48,50 m (159.28 ft); lenght 47,50 m (155.84 ft); height 12,20 m (40.02 ft); wing area 292,6 sq m (3,149.52 sq ft); undercarriage track about 12,25 m (40.19 ft).

Weights: Loaded 150.000 kg (330,700 lb); maximum take-off 168.000 kg (370,000 lb).

Performance: Maximum speed 881 km/h (547 mph) at 11.000 m (36,089 ft) (Mach 0,83); maximum cruise 807 km/h (501 mph) at 12.500 m (41,000 ft) (Mach 0,76); econ. cruise 711 km/h (442 mph) at 11.000 m (36,089 ft); service ceiling 13.500 m (44,300 ft); maximum range (without in-flight refuelling) 12.550 km (7,800 mls) with 5.000 kg/11,000 lb bombload, 6.450 km (4,000 mls) with 10.000 kg/22,000 lb bombload.

Armament: Six Nudelmann-Richter NR-23 23-mm cannons in three remotely-controlled turrets and 30.000 kg (66,000 lb) of free-fall nuclear and conventional bombs.

Tupolev Tu-22 (Blinder)

When, in 1961, the Tupolev Tu-22 medium bomber was officially presented it became a victim of mistaken identity. Before its real identity was ascertained it was attributed to Myasischev and Yakovlev.

Placed in the same class as the American B-58 (even if its performance is inferior), it is destined to replace the Tupolev-16, in turn classed with the American B-47.

The plans which complied with this request are not known (even if the Ilyushin Il-54 is similar it must be placed in an inferior category) but without a doubt the Blinder originated from the Tupolev Tu-98 (Backfin). To increase the confusion it was also erroneously identified as Yakovlev Yak-42. This aircraft basically had the Tu-16's airframe which had undergone some modifications and it was powered by two Lyulka AL-7Fs. The Tu-98 first flew in 1955, however the West first heard of it in 1957. The experience drawn from the Tu-98, which also reverted onto the Tu-102, caused the Tupolev OKB to draw up a plan, temporarily referred to as Samolet Yu (Yu aircraft, the last but one letter of the Russian alphabet) and later called Tu-105. The V-VS designated this project Tu-22 (previously attributed to a little known Tu-82 of 1949) and the prototypes probably flew between 1957 and 1960. Various engines have been mentioned with regards to their power plant: the Lyulka AL-7Fs, the Mikulin AM-3Ms or RD-3M-500s, the Soloviev D-15s.

The public first viewed the Tu-105/Tu-22 in July 1961 during the Moscow-Tushino Aviation Day (destined to remain as famous as the one held in 1967), in which nine pre-series or production

Top to bottom: the electronic warfare and reconnaissance Tu-22R (Blinder-C) with new partially retractable refuelling probe, six reconnaissance systems in the bomb bay and differentially operated tailplane. The crew of a reconnaissance Blinder. Maintenance routine around a Blinder-B.

The very first version of the Tu-22 (Blinder-A), without in-flight refuelling capability and with free-fall only bomb bay.

exemplars paraded along with one modified version armed with an AS-4 Kitchen air-to-surface missile. NATO observers called the Tu-22 Beauty, however, later renamed Blinder to comply with the ASCC rule which states that code names were not to be laudatory. The -A and -B prefixes were assigned by taking into consideration the role of the aircraft rather than the actual modifications it underwent: -A indicates the nuclear and conventional bombing configuration, -B indicates the missile armament configuration.

From a structural viewpoint, instead, an earlier version is identified, characterized by a front radome perfectly connected to the fuselage and without an in-flight refuelling probe, probably unsuitable for missile armament use (Tu-22 Blinder-A). Subsequently, the aircraft was equipped with a wider range attack radar, recognizable by an enlarged radome, a partially retractable in-flight refuelling probe and special bomb bay hatches which allow the use of free fall bombs as well as an air-to-surface missile (Tu-22 Blinder-B). By applying a new type of in-flight refuelling

probe and modifying the bomb bay to hold six photoelectronic systems and an ECM the Tu-22R (first indicated as Blinder-A and later Blinder-C) was created, while the Tu-22T (Blinder-C) version maintains combat capacities for maritime patrol and anti-ship attack — approximately 60 exemplars have been distributed to AV-MF units. There is also a training version, the Tu-22U (first Blinder-C and later Blinder-D) immediately recognizable for its raised pilot seat and an interception variation (up until the end of 1976 no pictures had ever been seen) called Tu-128/Tu-22P (Blinder-E), armed with four medium range air-to-air missiles which should be the AA-5 Ash model.

It is thought that only 230-320 Tupolev Tu-22s have ever been built. The word «failure» has often been used when speaking of the Blinder due to its insufficient range compared with that of the Tu-16 which it should have replaced. In fact, the Tu-22 — because of its very formula — has a reduced range of action and for this reason fewer models were built in comparison with sonic bom-

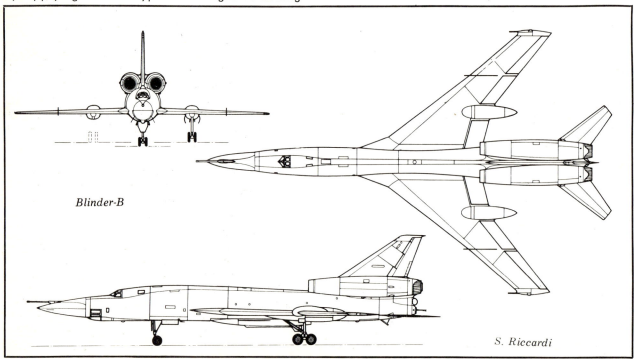

Blinder-B

S. Riccardi

bers; this same situation developed in the West with the American B-58s and the French Mirage IV-As whose production and use are or have been rather limited.

The airframe of the Tu-22 was possibly modified in order to give life to a prototype with variable geometric wings, created as test bed for the subsequent Backfire (classed with the American B-1) which seems to be the successor of the Blinder.

Operative Blinders are seldom encountered out of the Soviet Union. There has been talk of their exportation into Libya (a dozen) and of a request on behalf or Iraq, but only the former was verified in late 1976. They are rarely used as missile carriers and at present they are carrying out three principal duties; maritime patrol and anti-ship attack with conventional arms (in AV-MF units), conventional and nuclear tactical bombing of ground targets and electronic warfare. It is believed that they were used in this last role during the invasion of Czechoslovakia taking advantage of their passive ECM range. At the end of 1976 there were inclusively 170 Tu-22s in service in the USSR.

Tupolev Tu-105 Tu-22 (Blinder-B)
Tactical-strategic medium bomber, with 3 man crew

Power plant: Two 127,57 kN (13.000 kg/s, 28,660 lb/st) Soloviev D-15 turbofans. According to other sources the trust of the D-15 is 146,71 kN (14.950 kg/s, 32,960 lb). It is also possible the power plant is made of two Lyulka or AL-21F.
Dimensions: Wing span 26,85 m (88.09 ft); length 40,95 m (134.25 ft); height 11,00 m (36.09 ft); wing area about 188 sq m (2,023.6 sq ft) undercarriage track about 9,75 m (32 ft).
Weights: Maximum take-off 84.000 kg (185,000 lb).

Performance: Maximum speed (without ASM) 1.600 km/h (994 mph) at 12.000 m (39,300 ft) (Mach 1,5), 1.160 km/h (721 mph) at 300 m (1,000 ft) (Mach 0,95); cruise 960 km/h (596 mph) at 12.000 m (39,300 ft) (Mach 0,9); service ceiling 18.000 m (59,000 ft); combat radius 1.000-1.530 km (621-950 mls); range 2.250-3.670 km (1,398-2,280 mls).
Armament: One Nudelmann-Richter NR-23 23-mm cannon in radar-controlled tail turret and 10.000 kg (22,000 lb) of ordnance (typical 20 500 kg/1,100 lb-bombs or two H bombs) or one AS-4 Kitchen air-to-surface missile with 740 km/460 mls-range.

Tupolev Tu-26 (Backfire)

In 1962, period in which the Tupolev Tu-22 (Blinder) medium bomber began replacing the Tupolev Tu-16, Soviet military theory maintained that strategic targets located at the inferior border of intermediate distances (2,500-3,000 km 1,500-1,875 mls) could only be successfully hit with missiles; therefore, it seems logical to think that the Backfire project was created to complete the range of nuclear carriers, thereby, inserting itself among the aircraft and tactical short range missiles and the IRBMs, medium range intercontinentals.

In the autumn of 1969 information began leaking out on a new project which essentially concerned the conversion of a Tu-22 into a variable geometric wing aircraft according to the configuration formula already achieved on the Sukhoi Su-7 Fitter. In the West the aircraft was first referred to as Blinder-VG (Variable Geometry) and in July 1970 USAF reconnaissance satellites photographed a model which had just come out of production on an airport adjacent to the plant of the Tupolev collective staff in Kazan (Central Asia). It seems that two prototypes of the aircraft, in its original configuration, (called Backfire-A in NATO code and probably assigned the designation Tu-26) were again photographed in flight as well as on the ground and also while performing in-flight refuelling training exercises with Myasi-schev M-4 (Bison) air tankers. An initial pre-series production followed the two prototypes. Basing itself on all the information gathered by its intelligence service the USAF was soon able to make a wooden reproduction of the aircraft and to obtain approximate data and characteristics which should not be too distant from the real ones. The American department of defense nicknamed this aircraft Big Swinger (with reference to the F-111 also called Swinger). The Soviet V-VS designation remains uncertain but it could be Tu-30 (Backfire-B) for the production models. The Backfire is a large two-engined jet propelled by two double flow Kuznetsov NK-144 modified turbojets flanking the fuselage, with two large bidimensional variable geometric air intakes. The wing has a fixed section terminating with nacelles which lodge the landing gear and mobile tips with a variable swept between 20° to 55°. The design of this aircraft dates back to Alexei A. Tupolev, son of the late Andrei.

Towards the end of 1976 USAF intelligence services were able to reconstruct a new scale model of the production Backfire-B which presented numerous changes compared with the Backfire-A, the most visible being the installation of a principal landing gear with six wheels that is found in the thickness lining of the wing. The form and dimension of the air intakes should vary, also the wing should have a smaller surface and the vertical rudder a new design; it is certain that a posterior 30mm cannon exists. The electronic apparatus of the Tu-30 (Backfire-B) is made up of a guide radar, a navigation and Down Beat attack radar, (IFF SRZO-2 type), a Fan Tail radar for aiming the 30mm cannon, a «panoramic» Sirena 3 passive radar, all standard navigation electronic apparatus (Compass radio, altimeter radio, Doppler radar, calculator, etc.), besides a new type of inertial system for long distance navigation, probably used in connection with military satellites. Numerous passive devices are installed for electronic warfare as well as active disturb apparatus.

The armament consists of the already mentioned cannon and two air-to-surface AS-6 missiles hung from two wing pylons; the bomb bay can hold up to 8,000 kg (17.600 lbs) of nuclear arms or approximately 16.500 kg (36,350 lbs) of conventional bombs. The SA-6 missile has a maximum range of 800 km (500 mls). The aircraft's combat

range of action (including missile range) should be of 6.800 km (4,225 mls) on high altitude supersonic mission. With only one in-flight refuelling the aircraft's range of action increases to 8,700 km (5,400 mls) at supersonic velocity and to 10,000 km (6,200 mls) at an inferior velocity. Therefore, the maximum range should be 20,000 km (12,400 mls).

The first unit to be fitted with the Backfire-A should have been an ADD (Strategic Air Force) squadron formed by nine aircraft stationed in south-west Russia, followed by a second squadron of the AV-MF (Naval Air Force) under the Black Sea Command. Approximately 17 exemplars, including the two prototypes and the first production Backfire-B, should have been used in crew training. According to American information at least two ADD regiments should already be equipped with the new aircraft and a third should be forming. At the end of 1976 flight lines included approximately 80 Backfire-Bs aircraft effectively in service but which had since then only completed training flights without external loads.

Tupolev Tu-26/30 (?) (Backfire-B)
Strategic medium bomber with 3 man crew

Power plant: Two 127,57 kN (13.000 kg/st, 28,660 lb/st) dry and 196.27 kN (20,000 kg/st, 44,000 lb/st) reheat Kuznetsov NK-144 double shaft turbofans.
Fuel capacity: (extimated) 68.000 kg (149,900 lb) or about 85.200 l (18,740 gal).
Dimensions: Wing span (20°) 34,50 m (113.19 ft), (55°) 26,20 m (85.96 ft); length 40,20 m (131.89 ft); height 10,0 m (32,81 ft); wing area 134,5-168 sq m (1,447.75-1,808.33 sq ft).
Weights: Empty 47.000 kg (103,615 lb); maximum take-off 122.500 kg (270,00 lb).
Performance: Maximum speed 2.123 km/h (1.319 mph) at 11.000 m (36,089 ft) (Mach 2,0), 1.102

km/h (685 mph) at sea level (Mach 0,9); initial climb rate 140 m/sec (27,500 ft/min); service ceiling above 18.000 m (59,000 ft); combat radius 2.500-6.000 km (1,550-3,730 mls); 8.700 km (5,400 mls) with one in-flight refuelling; range 6.000-14.400 km (3,730-8,950 mls); maximum still air range over 20.000 km (12,400 mls) without in-flight refuelling.
Armament: One Nudelmann-Richter NR-30 30-mm cannon in radarcontrolled tail turret, two hardpoints for AS-4 Kitchen or AS-6 ASM missiles and bomb bay for 8.000 kg (17,600 lb) of nuclear or conventional free-fall bombs (one-two megaton-class thermonuclear bombs, at least four 350 kiloton tactical nuclear bombs or 16.500 kg/36,350 lb conventional bombs.

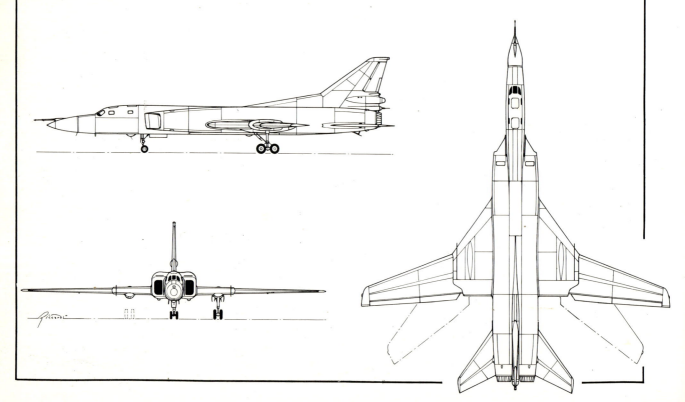

Helicopters

Mil Mi-4 (Hound)

One of the most widely used Soviet helicopters, the Mil Mi-4 (or V-4 for the Armed Forces; V for Vertolet, helicopter), evolved from the Sikorsky formula with a four or five-blade main rotor and a tail antitorque rotor. It is comparable to the western S-55s and the S-58s Wessex with regards to its dimensions and use and it can transport 14 soldiers or 1,700 kg (3,750 lbs) of payload. Destined to be progressively replaced with the Mil Mi-8, it has just recently been phased-out by the AV-MF but is still in service with the V-VS, the KGB and the Border Police.

Mil Mi-4 V-4 (Hound, former Type 36)
Tactical transport helicopter

Power plant: one 1.700 HP (emergency) or 1.430-1.530 HP (continuous) Shvetsov ASh-82V, 14 cylinder air-cooled radial engine.
Dimensions: Rotor diameter 21,0 m (68.90 ft); fuselage length 16,80 m (55.12 ft); height 5,18 m (16.99 ft); rotor disc area 346 sq m (3,724.31 sq ft).
Weights: Empty 5.268 kg (11,650 lb); loaded 7.500 kg (16,500 lb); maximum take-off 7.800 kg (17,200 lb).

Performance: Maximum speed 210 km/h (130 mph) at 1.500 m (4,920 ft); economical cruise 160 km/h (99 mph); service ceiling 5.500 m (18,000 ft); range (with 1.000 kg/2,200 lb payload) 250 km (155 mls); maximum range 595 km (370 mls).

Armament: (optional) one Kalashnikov RPK 7,62 mm machine-gun or (ASW) sonobuoys, ASW devices and depth charges or torpedos.

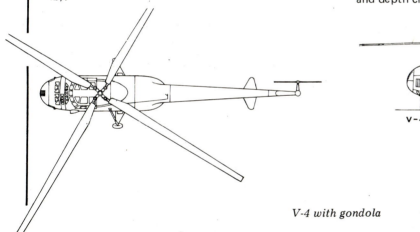

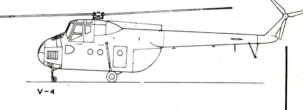

V-4

V-4 with gondola

Mil Mi-6 (Hook)

In 1955, the Soviet Armed Forces were the first to require heavy lift helicopter which would replace their Yakovlev Yak-24 and be capable of transporting the same payload as that of a tactical transport aircraft. The prototype first flew in 1957, and in the summer of 1961 the first 30 exemplars of production began to be distributed to the units. This aircraft can also be paralleled to the Sikorsky S-61, but its dimensions (and capacity) are far superior. Besides, the production version is, in effect, a winged helicopter in as much as it mounts a true wing with a span of 15.30m (50.19 ft). The Mi-6 should have been replaced by the Mi-12, truly the «Jumbo-helicopter».

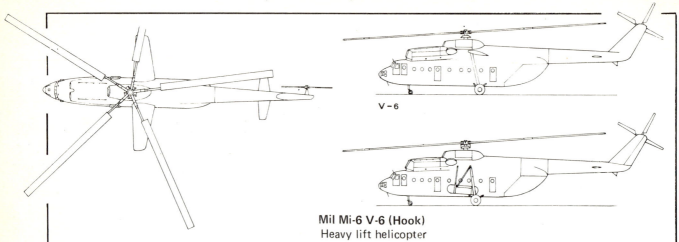

Mil Mi-6 V-6 (Hook)
Heavy lift helicopter

Power plant: Two 4.101 kW (5,500 HP) Soloviev D-25V (TV-2BM) turboshaft engine.
Dimensions: Rotor diameter 35,00 m (114.83 ft); overall length (rotors turning) 41,74 m (136.94 ft); fuselage length 33,18 m (108.86 ft); height 9,86 m (32.35 ft.)
Weights: Empty 27.240 kg (60,055 lb); loaded 40.500 kg (89,285 lb); maximum take-off weight with slung load 37.500 kg (82,675 lb); maximum take-off weight (vertical) 42.500 kg (93,700 lb).
Performance: Maximum speed 300 km/h (186 mph); maximum cruise 250 km/h (155 km/h); service ceiling 4.500 m (14,750 ft); range 650-1.050 km (404-652 mls); ferry range 1.450 km (900 mls).

Mil Mi-8 (Hip) and derivatives

The Mil Mi-8 (or V-8) can be considered a turbine derivation of the above. Development of the V-8 went on from 1958 to September 17, 1962 when the prototype flew in final configuration. This helicopter can transport either 24 fully equipped soldiers, 32 passengers without baggage or 24 wounded on stretchers and beginning with 1967 it became the standard helicopter of all the Soviet Armed Forces. The possibility of transporting armaments such as four UV-16-57 rocket-launchers, totalling 64 unguided 57 mm rockets or four wire guided antitank AT-3 Sagger missiles and one Degtyarev RPD or Kalashnikov RPK 7,62 mm machine gun firing across the left front door was introduced around 1971.

This version was adopted while waiting for the development of a real combat helicopter, the V-24 (Hind), which has been known to the West since 1972 and which entered service in East Germany in 1973, however no photographs were available until 1974.

The development period of the above is paralled to two other variations: one which was able to install pontoons and was used by the Navy «Black Berets» for landing operations and one (V-14 Haze) for antisubmarine combat. The first information on this was carried by the Italian aeronautical press in June 1973.

The V-24 (Hind-A), classed with the ill-fated Sikorsky Blackhawk, must also be considered an interim combat version, and in 1975 the final versions were built: the A-10, (Hind-C and -D), the former of which entered service with the Soviet Armed Forces in Germany at the beginning of 1977.

Even though the Hind-A (NATO had mistakenly identified it as the Hind-B pre-series version, mistaking it for a developed version), offers remarkable armament possibilities, it remains an assault helicopter, maintaining the possibility of transporting at least eight soldiers. On the other hand, the Hind-D is a combat helicopter equipped with a «visionic» system and armament made up of a turret with a new type gun having three or four rotating barrels and a calibre between 7,62 and 14,5 mm. It reaches a maximum speed of 330-340 km/h (205-211 mph).

Mil Mi-8 V-8 (Hip)
Tactical transport helicopter

Power plant: Two 1.118 kW (1,500 HP) Isotov TV-2-117A turboshaft engines.
Dimensions: Rotor diameter 21,29 m (69.85 ft); overall length (rotors turning) 25,28 m (82.94 ft); fuselage length 18,31 m (60.07 ft); height 5,60 m (18.37 ft); rotor disc area 355 sq m (3,821 sq ft).
Weights: Empty 6.816 kg (15,026 lb); loaded 11.100 kg (24,470 lb); maximum take-off with slung load 11.430 kg (25,200 lb); maximum take-off (vertical) 12.000 kg (26,455 lb).
Performance: Maximum speed 250 km/h (155 mph), with slung load 180 km/h (119 mph); maximum cruise 225 km/h (140 mph); service ceiling 4.500 m (14,760 ft), in hovering in ground effect 1.800 m (5.900 ft), out of g.e. 800 m (2,625 ft); range 100-475 km (62-295 mls); ferry range 940 km (584 mls).
Armament: as noted above (optional).

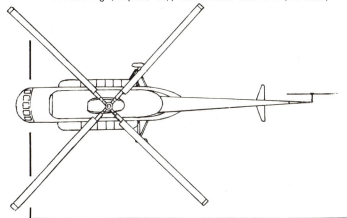

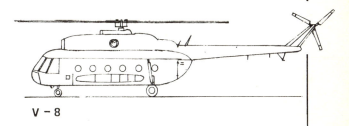

V - 8

Naval Aviation

YAKOVLEV YAK-36 (FORGER)
In 1967 the Soviets presented a prototype of a fighter V/STOL aircraft at Domodedovo which was called Freehand by the West. In the following years another Soviet V/STOL was identified by the Americans, temporarily called RAM-G which, was thought, would be based on the *Kiev*-class carrier. However even this aircraft was abandoned and in 1969 a new project took shape which would bring us to the present Forger — a VTOL carrier-based aircraft exclusively destined for the *Kievs* (*Kuril* according to the NATO code), and which should be their only type of fixed wing aircraft.

The Yak-36, (the same initials were already mentioned with regards to the Freehand) was credited to the Yakovlev «collective», but it is probably the result of collaboration between at least two different Soviet engineering staffs.

The principal role of the Yak-36 (Forger-A) is anti-ship attack at low altitude with an aptitude limited to the air defense of naval units. The wings are foldable at approximately midspan to facilitate the on board hangarage.

Besides the single-seat version, a two-seat training version has been created — the Yak-36U (Forger-B) — with tandem two-seat, having a longer front portion by about 1.60 - 1.80 m (5.25 - 5.90 ft) than the preceeding version. Yakovlev's VTOL fighter-bomber will be based on all the units of the Kiev-class carriers but the total number of aircraft per unit is still uncertain: officially 12 Yak-36s are spoken of, but western estimates ascend to possibly 15-20 or even 24 aircraft.

Yakovlev Yak-36 (?) (Forger-A)
VTOL carrierborne fighter-bomber, single seat

Power plant: One axial turbojet exhausting through two of vectoring nozzle in the 8.000 kg/17,600 lb/st class reduced to 7.200 kg/s (15,875 lb/st) in the VTOL mode (possibly a modified Lyulka AL-21 without reheat and two 3.600 kg/st (7,930 lb/st) lift-jets of unspecified type. Fuel capacity: (extimated) 3.000 l (660 gal).

Dimensions: Wing span 8,83 m (28.97 ft), (wing folded) 5,55 m (18.21 ft); length 14,66 m (48.10 ft); height 4,15 m (13.61 ft); wing span 20,60 sq m (221.73 sq ft).

Weights: Empty (equipped) 6.250 kg (13,780 lb); loaded 8.650 kg (19,070 lb); maximum take-off (vertical) 10.000 kg (22,000 lb).

Performance: Maximum speed 1.286 km/h (799 mph) at sea level (Mach 1,05); cruise 850 km/h (528 mph) at low level; initial climb rate 75 m/sec (14,775 ft/min); service ceiling 12.000 m (39,300 ft); combat radius 425 km (264 mls); range 1.060 km (658 mls).

Armament: 1.000 kg (2,200 lb) of ordnance.

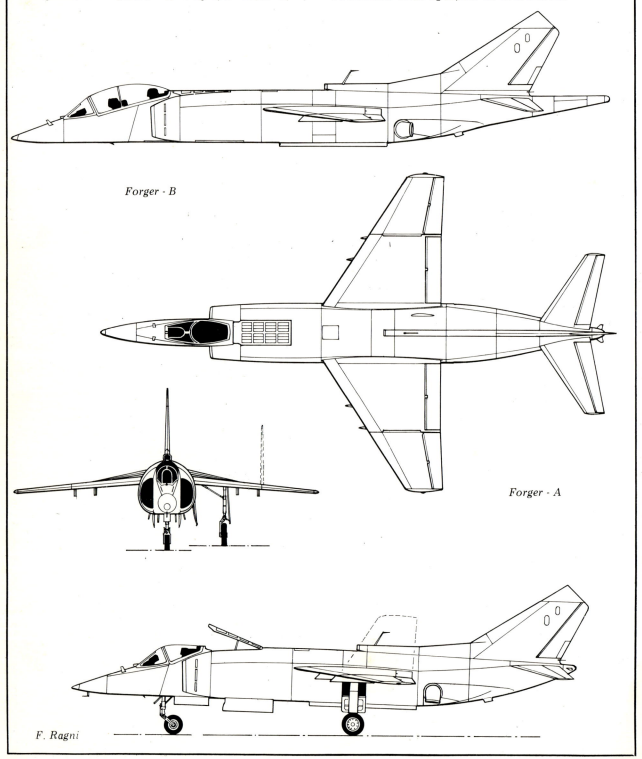

Forger - B

Forger - A

F. Ragni

BERIEV BE-12 TCHAIKA (MAIL)

This model was presented at Tushino in 1961 and was considered a simple rework of the Be-6's (Madge) with turboprop engines even if it appears to have been completely redesigned and it is an amphibian rather than a conventional flying boat. It seems to have been planned around 1958 as a reserve program against the possible failure of the two-engined Be-10 jet and replacement of the Be-6. It probably flew as a prototype in 1960 or the beginning of 1961.

It is also believed that the Tchaika (seagull), officially called M-12 by the Soviet Navy and Mail in the West, entered service in 1963-1965, and by 1967, when it had more complete exposure at the Domodedovo Aviation Day, large numbers were already in service.

At present, together with the Grumman HU-16B

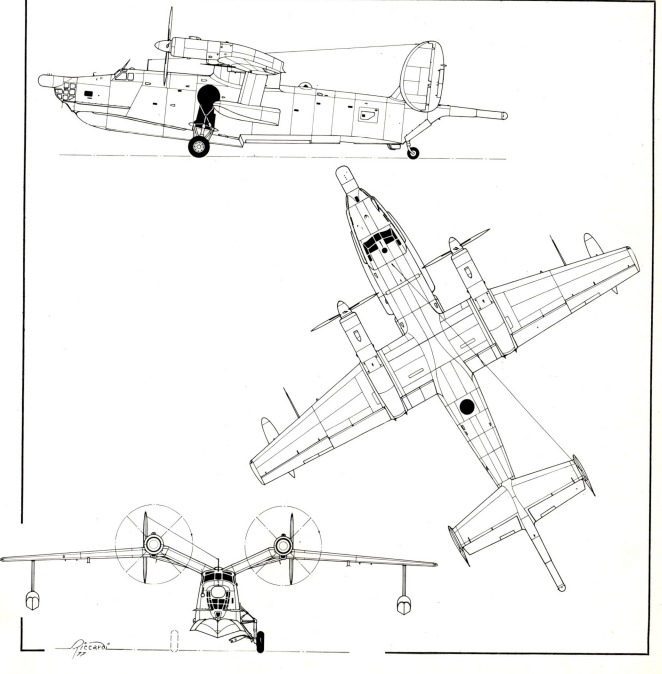

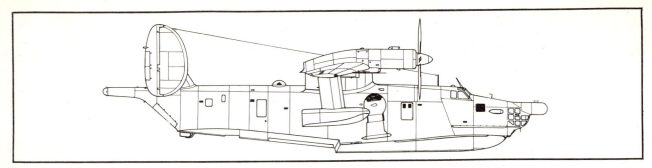

Albatross and the Shin Meiwa SS-1 it represents the category of the anti-submarine amphibians and it is serving, in particular, the *Red Flag* Fleets in the Black Sea, the North Sea and the Pacific with over 100 exemplars. It does not give the impression of being particularly well furnished with an AS instrumentation: a rather small diametered search radar, and a MAD detector lodges in the semiretractable tail «stinger». The armament is housed in a bomb day immediately behind the «redan» of the hull and it is sustained by two wing hardpoints suitable only for reduced weight loads. Towards the tail there are ASW devices.

This aircraft has collected an incredible number of class (Class C.3, G.3 Group II, C.2 Group II) and individual records that it is impossible to list them all; among the most important are; in October 1964 the M. Mikhailov, I. Kuprianov and L. Kuznetsov crew climb to 12,185 m, 9,352 m with a payload of 10,000 kg and 2,000 m with 10,000 kg; on April 25, 1968 E. Nikitin averaged 565,347 km/h on a closed circuit of 500 km; on November 20, 1973 G. Efimov covers the distance on a closed circuit of 2,581.62 km; in November 1974 A. Zacharov climbs to 3,000 m in five minutes 6.2 seconds and E. Nikitin climbs to 6,000 m in 11 minutes and 57.4 seconds; and

finally, on April 28 and 29, 1975 Avershin climbs to 8,223 m reaching 9,000 m in 22 minutes 9.8 seconds.

During production the search and navigation radar antenna changed from a paraboloid to an elongated shaped one.

Beriev Be-12 M-12 Tchaika (Mail)
Amphibious ASW patrol aircraft with five man crew

Power plant: Two 3.171 kW (4.309 CV, 4.250 HP) Ivchenko AI-20M turboprops. Propellers: Two AV-681 metal four blade reversible pitch of 4,50 m (14.76 ft) diameter.
Dimensions: Wing span 29,67 m (97.34 ft); length 33,22 m (108.99 ft); height (propellers turning) 9,66 m (31.69 ft), (top of the tail) 7,40 m (24.28 ft); wing area 95,7 sq m (1,030,1 sq ft); undercarriage track 5,56 m (18.24 ft).
Weights: Empty 19.500 kg (42,990 lb); maximum take-off 29.600 kg (65,255 lb).
Performance: Maximum speed 610 km/h (379 mph) at 3.000 m (9.840 ft); maximum continuous speed 565 km/h (351 mph); patrol speed 320 km/h (199 mph) at 300 m (1,000 ft); initial climb rate 15 m/sec (2,950 ft/min); service ceiling 8.200 m (26,900 ft); absolute ceiling 12.185 m (39,975 ft); combat radius 1.000 km (620 mls); maximum range 2.500-4.000 km (1,550-2,485 mls).
Armament: 2.000 kg (4,400 lb) of ASW armament (including two torpedoes).

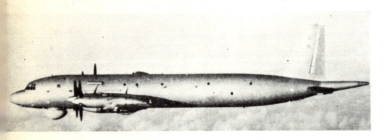

ILYUSHIN IL-38 (MAY)

The plans to develope a jet patrol aircraft (the Be-10,which was withdrawn from service in 1965) fell through because of the limited range of the Be-12,estimated by the West between 1,000 and 4,000 km and nevertheless insufficient for oceanic patrol. Therefore, the Soviet Navy requested a new aircraft which, according to a solution by this time widespread in the West, would be stationed on ground, would offer a remarkable autonomy together with the capacity of remaining in the air for at least 12 hours and would derive from an already existing airframe.

Following the example set by Lockheed, Ilyushin and Novozilov decided to work on an already existing aircraft, their Il-18D Moskva (Coot), long range version of the 100 seat commercial four turboprops aircraft.

The project evolved around 1966 and it is believed to have given origin to aerodynamic prototypes which also happened in the Electra/Orion case. So that heavy loads and equipment could be carried on board the wing was shifted ahead with respect to the fuselage in order to recover the gravity centre to its proper position, and even though the basic design of the Il-18 was maintained, some redesigning was necessary especially within the interior.

The prototype of the Il-38 (May for the NATO) most likely flew in 1968 (or late 1967) and in 1970 the first operative Il-38s were already noted in the Mediterranean and particularly on all the Soviet seas. For a certain period a detachment of Il-38s also operated from Egypt and during that period the aircraft, even though belonging to the

Soviet MF, flew with individual codes in Arabic numbers and Egyptian insignias.

The II-38 is still an almost unknown aircraft and at present it is only serving in the USSR even if it has been offered to the Indian Navy which has ordered three and has taken an option for another three.

The avionics include a large search radar under the nose, a MAD detector (obviously in the tail) and several other instruments (among which those for processing signals transmitted by sonobuoys) whose presence is betrayed by various antennas and dielectrics in the fuselage. Little is known about the armament, but English sources speak of three bays under the flight deck, in the fuselage, one or two of which are used to hold AS devices (smoke markers, sonobuoys, etc.), while four wing hardpoints, which have actually never been seen installed, could carry ECM containers, rockets and rocket-launchers.

At the end of 1976 there were about 80 II-38s serving in the USSR.

KAMOV KA-25 (HORMONE-A)

The Soviet Navy's standard helicopter is the Kamov Ka-25. This is a rather compact aircraft featuring two three-blade counterrotating rotors typical of Nikolai I. Kamov's production and is suitable for carrierborne stowage. The «marine» and ASW equipment includes emergency inflatable pontoons, search radar in a «chin» radome, dunking sonar, and a towed magnetic anomaly detector; an added avionics system and an electro-optical sensor appear on certain models. The armament, contained in a ventral bay, comprises ASW torpedoes, depth charges, etc.

At present, the Ka-25s fit out all the Soviet ships equipped with flight deck and they are flanked by a small number of Mil Mi-6s and Mi-8s for landing and command operations and they have initiated replacement on the principal ships or in ground units by the Mi-14s (Haze), all-weather ASW helicopters comparable to the western Sikorsky Sea Kings.

Kamov Ka-25 (Hormone-A)
Ship-based ASW helicopter, with three-four man crew

Power plant: Two 662 kW (900 HP) Glushenkov GTD-3 turboshaft engines.
Dimensions: Rotors diameter 15,74 m (51.64 ft); overall length (rotors turning) 15,74 m (51.64 ft); fuselage length (without «radome» and antennas) 9,83 m (32.25 ft.); height (rotors hub) 5,37 m (17.62 ft); rotor disc area 194,5 sq m (2,093.4 sq ft).
Weights: Empty 4.600 kg (10,150 lb); Maximum take-off 7.300 kg (16,100 lb).
Performance: Maximum speed 220 km/h (137 mph); cruise 193 km/h (120 mph); service ceiling 3.500 m (11,500 ft); range 400 km (250 mls), (maximum fuel) 600-650 km (372-405 mls).
Armament: (approx.) 1.800 kg (3,970 lb) of ASW ordnance.

Ilyushin II-38 (May)
Long range ASW patrol aircraft, land based, with 12 man crew

Power plant: Four 3.171 kW (4.309 CV, 4.250 HP) Ivchenko AI-20M turboprops. Propellers: Four AV-681 metal four blade reversible pitch of 4,50 m (14.76 ft) diameter. Fuel capacity: 23.700 l (5,213 gal) in wing tanks; other tanks of unknown capacity are in the fuselage and central wing section.
Dimensions: Wing span 37,40 m (122,70 ft); length 39,75 m (130.41 ft); height 10,17 m (33.36 ft); wing area 140 sq m (1,506.95 sq ft); undercarriage track 9,0 m (29.52 ft).
Weights: Empty 36.300 kg (80,000 lb); maximum take-off 64.000 kg (14,100 lb).
Performance: Maximum speed 715-760 km/h (444-472 mph); maximum cruise 645 km/h (401 mph) at 4.500 m (14,760 ft); economic cruise 595 km/h (369 mph) at 8.000 m (26,250 ft); patrol speed 400 km/h (248 mph) at 600 m (2,000 ft); combat radius (at 645 km/h/401 mph) 2.870 km (1,780 mls); range 7.170 km (4,455 mls); endurance 12-18 h.
Armament: approx. 2.800 kg (6,170 lb) of torpedoes, depth charges, mines, air-to-surface rockets, etc.

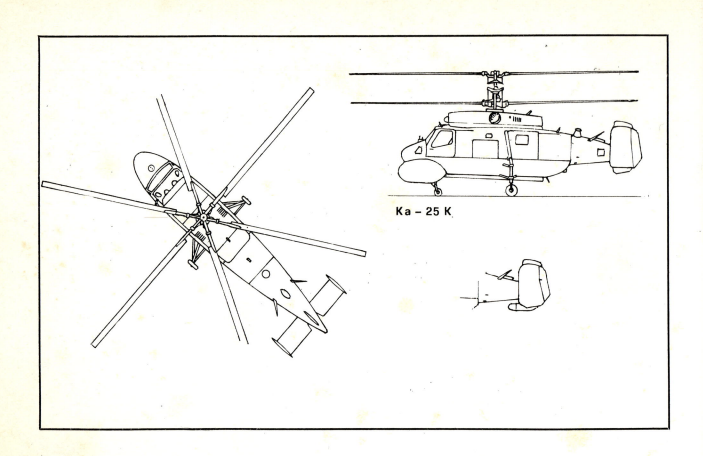

Ka – 25 K